Making Out in Japanese

by Todd Geers & Erika Hoburg
Revised Edition by Glen McCabe
with the invaluable assistance of
Hiromi Fumoto, Kazu Wada,
Hiroko Irita, Nobu Kanno,
Tama Kanayama and Etsuko Sato

Illustrations by Erika Hoburg

TUTTLE Publishing

Tokyo | Rutland, Vermont | Singapore

Published by Tuttle Publishing, an imprint of Periplus Editions (HK) Ltd.

www.tuttlepublishing.com

LCC Card No. 88050165
ISBN 978-0-8048-3396-7
ISBN 978-4-8053-0712-0 (for sale in Japan only)

Printed in Singapore

Distributed by:

Japan
Tuttle Publishing, Yaekari Building 3F
5-4-12 Osaki, Shinagawa-ku
Tokyo 141-0032, Japan
Tel: (81) 3 5437 0171
Fax: (81) 3 5437 0755
sales@tuttle.co.jp
www.tuttle.co.jp

North America, Latin America & Europe
Tuttle Publishing
364 Innovation Drive,
North Clarendon VT 05759-9436, USA
Tel: 1 (802) 773 8930
Fax: 1 (802) 773 6993
info@tuttlepublishing.com
www.tuttlepublishing.com

Asia Pacific
Berkeley Books Pte. Ltd.
61 Tai Seng Avenue #02-12
Singapore 534167
Tel: (65) 6280-1330
Fax: (65) 6280-6290
inquiries@periplus.com.sg
www.periplus.com

15 14 13 12 11   1106CP
15 14 13 12 11

Contents

Introduction

So no one understands your Japanese? Worse yet, you don't understand theirs. You've spent an entire week studying one phrase and you can't wait to use it. The big moment arrives— you're armed with the latest edition of *Learn Japanese in 27-and-a-1/2-Minutes-a-Day* for moral support—and you lay the phrase on some unsuspecting soul. What happens? The response isn't like the one in your book. Why?

Basically, because the Japanese don't "play by the book" just as Westerners don't "play by the book" when it comes to their daily language. So what to do? Well, you could quit and give up studying Japanese, or you could learn to speak real Japanese.

Just as we speak in a relaxed, colloquial manner, so do the Japanese. On trains, in clubs, during ball games, or with friends, they all use shortcuts in their speech. If you want to speak the way the Japanese speak, then you need to know what to say, how to say it, and when to say it.

And better still, you'll need to know the cultural context it all happens in. We've built in lots of little morsels in this book to help you build a picture of the real Japan as you go along. Right then? Okay, let's go!

INFORMATION

It's tricky to teach the proper pronunciation of a foreign language in a book, so we're not going to try, hoping you've already got the basics. To help you out, though, we've joined two and sometimes three or four words together, to make compound words or phrases that are easier to pronounce. Most of them are hyphenated to highlight merged words, to emphasize the slang suffixes and particles, and to facilitate pronunciation and memorization.

For example, the components of *fuzakenaide-yo* （ふざけないでよ） are: *fuzake* (from *fuzakeru*), *naide* (command form of *arimasen*), and the (quite forceful) suffix -*yo*. We've written the compound phrase *fuzakenaide-yo* so that you won't pause while pronouncing it, but say it entirely in one breath; a pause would weaken the impact.

We're sure that you're familiar with the polite question forms *des-ka* ですか and *mas-ka* ますか. Forget them. Except for a few needed for talking to strangers, requesting services, etc., the rest have been dismissed. In informal speech, rising intonation takes the place of these forms. Thus, the final syllables of all words and phrases in this book ending with a question mark should be pronounced with the kind of rising intonation we give to the question "Right?"

Slang that is too faddish is not included in this book, because such words come and go too quickly. If you use old slang, the reaction of your Japanese date will likely be, "He thinks he's being cool speaking like that, but nobody says that anymore. Hah, hah!" So we've avoided hot slang—if it's out of date people will think that you're funny or square. But feel free to use what you pick up on the street.

VARIATIONS

The terms "boy" and "girl" are used throughout the book, and we're definitely referring to the post-puberty phase here. To eliminate the embarrassing problem of boys using girls' words or vice versa, we've indicated words suitable for use by girls and boys with the symbols ♀ and ♂ respectively. Other words and phrases not marked can be used by both sexes, and (b→g) means a boy should use it when talking to a girl. For example:

Don't be upset.	Okoranaide. ♂
	おこ怒らないで。
	Okoruna-yo. ♀
	おこ怒るなよ。
Make me warm.	Atatamete.
	暖めて。
You look beautiful.	Kirei-dayo. (b→g)
	きれいだよ。

But before you go thinking that boys' and girls' speech patterns are absolutely divided, stop a minute. Don't be shocked if you hear a girl using a quite masculine phrase (or vice versa). The gender gap in Japanese speech is narrowing, especially among young people, and there's nothing wrong with "borrowing" for impact or emphasis. In this book, we've made the distinction as a general guide to usage.

One thing you'll notice as you speak with the Japanese (especially if you move around) is that people's speech patterns vary wildly. We're not just talking about slang here, there are also big differences between regions and social groups. It's impossible for us to include all the variations (more on the regional ones later) of the phrases in this book, so we've gone a standard Japanese (*hyojungo* 標準語) style, which everyone will understand and which you can adapt to the area you're living in.

Adaptation is really important—the phrases here might seem too harsh to some ears and too soft to others. Take your cues from the speech and reactions of people around you. If they warm to the way you're talking, great, otherwise think about the way they're taking it and adjust. If all else fails, ask—foreigners aren't expected to know everything!

JAPANESE–ENGLISH–JAPANESE–...

You'll have seen above that we've written Japanese phrases in two ways—in *rōmaji* (ローマ字—Western script, with lines above some vowels meaning long sounds) and in Japanese script with *furigana* (phonetic *hiragana* 平仮名 above the Chinese *kanji* 漢字) for an added challenge as you get better. But many phrases are written in another phonetic alphabet, *katakana* 片仮名. *Katakana* are mostly used for foreign words, and there are many of them in this book —for example, "batteries" are *batterii* バッテリー. Among other things, they're also used to write a few Japanese superlatives, such as *chō* チョー (amazing-ly/fantastic-ally).

When using *katakana,* life gets a bit tricky when you hit the limitations of the Japanese language. It has only one final consonant (n), so when the Japanese pronounce English words with other consonant endings, they have to tack on a vowel, usually a *u.* "Game" becomes *gēmu* ゲーム, "bed" becomes *beddo* ベッド, etc. With no final "r" sound, they usually use a long "a"—for example "locker" becomes *rokkā* ロッカー. And since there is no "l" at all, "r" is used instead.

There are a few introduced sounds that the Japanese can usually pronounce, and so they've created new ways of writing them. A "we" (as in "web") is written ウェ, and v sounds are written as ヴ followed by a katakana vowel, as in *va* ヴァ, *vi* ヴィ etc.— though the ability to pronounce the *v* varies greatly, especially between generations!

The Japanese enjoy using English words sporadically in their speech and you should do the same. With a little practice, it's easy to get the hang of how to "*katakana-ize*" an English word, that is, to pronounce it the way a Japanese would, strange as it might seem at first. As a foreigner, you'd be expected to use *katakana* words—so don't hold back!

As a reference point, here's a chart of the 45 *kana* in each alphabet, with the *hiragana* listed first under each sound. There are various ways of writing some kana in *romaji* (e.g. *tu* or *tsu*)—we've gone with those closest to the sound.

a	あ	ア	i	い	イ	u	う	ウ	e	え	エ	o	お	オ
ka	か	カ	ki	き	キ	ku	く	ク	ke	け	ケ	ko	こ	コ
ga	が	ガ	gi	ぎ	ギ	gu	ぐ	グ	ge	げ	ゲ	go	ご	ゴ
sa	さ	サ	shi	し	シ	su	す	ス	se	せ	セ	so	そ	ソ
za	ざ	ザ	ji	じ	ジ	zu	ず	ズ	ze	ぜ	ゼ	zo	ぞ	ゾ
ta	た	タ	chi	ち	チ	tsu	つ	ツ	te	て	テ	to	と	ト
da	だ	ダ	ji	ぢ	ヂ	zu	づ	ヅ	de	で	デ	do	ど	ド
na	な	ナ	ni	に	ニ	nu	ぬ	ヌ	ne	ね	ネ	no	の	ノ
ha	は	ハ	hi	ひ	ヒ	fu	ふ	フ	he	へ	ヘ	ho	ほ	ホ
ba	ば	バ	bi	び	ビ	bu	ぶ	ブ	be	べ	ベ	bo	ぼ	ボ
pa	ぱ	パ	pi	ぴ	ピ	pu	ぷ	プ	pe	ぺ	ペ	po	ぽ	ポ
ma	ま	マ	mi	み	ミ	mu	む	ム	me	め	メ	mo	も	モ
ya	や	ヤ				yu	ゆ	ユ				yo	よ	ヨ
ra	ら	ラ	ri	り	リ	ru	る	ル	re	れ	レ	ro	ろ	ロ
wa	わ	ワ										o	を	ヲ
va		ヴァ	vi		ヴィ	vu		ヴ	ve		ヴェ	vo	ヴォ	

There are a few more variations in readings to watch out for. Notables are the use of *ha* as the subject particle, in which case it's read *wa* (such as *watashi-wa* 私は), and verbs ending in *-masu* ます, which we've romanised to *-mas*, because that's how you say it. You'll pick them all up as you go along.

BEING CHOOSY

There are plenty of phrases for which the Japanese have alternatives, as in any language. As well as the boy/girl classification, we've listed them in a rough order from least to most casual, also getting rougher as they become more casual. If what you're saying doesn't seem to fit the mood, again, adapt to the speech of the people around you!

In the book, we've included the Japanese words for "me" and "you" in many phrases. In practice, they often leave them out, unless particular clarification is needed, but until you can instinctively understand who is being referred to, it's best to use them. If you do, there are a range of words available, not just the gender-neutral *watashi* 私 (with its super-formal counterpart *watakushi* 私) and *anata* あなた that textbooks love.

For girls, there's *atashi* あたし, and for guys there's *boku* 僕 and *ore* 俺. To say "you," girls can say *anata* あなた or *anta* あんた, and guys can say *kimi* 君 or *omae* 前. In this book, we've stuck with *anata* and *kimi*, because these are the "safest" for everyday conversation. *Omae* and *ore* in particular are very harsh, uncompromising words that can put people off. Until you know when best to use these words (again by the speech of the Japanese around you), steer clear!

STRESSED OUT OVER ENDINGS

One thing that we have to say is that in Japanese, how you say something can have more meaning that what you say. Think about it: when you're sharing an intimate moment, you can convey many emotions by sounding caring and serious, on top of what you're actually saying. Some phrases can be changed from statements to questions just by the tone or particle at the end... the list goes on. Here's a run-down of some slang endings and tonal tricks.

For starters, the rules say that plain negative verbs end in -nai (e.g. wakaranai 分からない I don't understand/know). But you'll hear other forms, like -n, as in wakaran 分からん, or shiran 知らん (I dunno) or special corruptions like wakannai 分かんない and iu 言う pronounced yū ゆう. (Plain positive forms generally don't change as they're pretty simple already).

The most common slang final particle is ne, often lengthened to nē. Only partly fictitiously, it seems to us that when a newborn Japanese baby is shown off for the first time, someone will say Kawaii-nē? かわいいねえ？ (Isn't he/she cute?), and inevitably the flock of admirers will all say Nē! ねえ！ (Oh yes!). From such early exposure, the child is doomed to utter nē for the rest of his/her life.

Nē gives an (familiar yet) emphatic ending, usually a rhetorical question, and lengthening it adds more emphasis. With falling intonation it's more of an explanation. It isn't often said with a rising intonation, but can be said in a high pitch for emphasis. Girls prefer ne and nē, and guys have an alternative, na, which is used in the same way. But as we said before, the gap is narrowing, and, especially around women, guys will often use ne.

Other handy sentence endings (added to any form but the mas form) include yo よ, used to emphasise that "I'm telling you what I think (and you should do this)." Wa わ is often added by women to soften phrases, and you'll see it throughout this book. If you prefer a more blunt style, don't use it, or use yo instead. -noda 〜のだ (less formally -nda 〜んだ) makes the sentence a clear explanation, with a feeling, of "that's the way it is."

These can be combined liberally. For example, you're trying to decide which movie to see, and someone is being quite pushy about their choice. To be clear that you've already seen it and once was enough, you can say *Mō mitan-dayone* もう見たんだよね。

Zo ぞ and *ze* ぜ can be added (usually by guys) to give instructions. *Zo* means "let's do..." as in *Yoshi, iku-zo* よし、行くぞ (Right, let's go), similar to but slightly harsher than *iko* 行こう. *Ze* is a very strong command form, e.g. *Iku-ze!* 行くぜ！ (Move it!) Finally, *-kke* is a handy ending, expressing either uncertainty or forgetfulness *Nan-datta-kke?* 何だったっけ？ (What was it again...?)

The meaning of some phrases may be changed from a statement to a question by a rising final intonation, and these phrases are marked by diamonds (◆). For example:

Haven't seen you around for a while.

◆ Hisashiburi-ne. ♀
久しぶりね。
◆ Hisashiburi-dane.
久しぶりだね。

With a rising intonation, the sentence becomes "Haven't seen you around for a while, have I?"

And which parts of the phrase you stress also make a big difference—stressing a *yo* emphasizes that you're pushing your opinion. Stressing the *so* in *so-dane/so desu-ne* そうだね/そうですね (that's right) means you agree more strongly.

Finally, put emotion into your voice. You might think that the Japanese spoken around you is emotionless because it seems so fast, but nothing could be further from the truth. Put feeling into your voice as you would in English, and your message will be loud and clear.

THE LAST WORD

Does all of this sound really daunting? It shouldn't! Think of this introduction as a reference page for your journey through the Japanese-speaking world. Just keep these points in mind, and you'll find this book a valuable resource to speed your street Japanese skills along.

And there's one last thing: the Japanese love to see foreigners making an effort to speak Japanese! Through their troubles learning English, they know how hard it is, so even if you can't get the point across to start with, keep trying and you'll earn more respect. And if you're using real phrases like the ones in this book, all the better!

What's Up? 1

Hello! Hi!

Ohayo!
おはよう！
Konnichi-wa!
こんにちは！
Komban-wa!
こんばんは！

Ohayo! is used in the morning, say until 10 a.m., and with people you're seeing for the first time that day. *Konnichi-wa!* is for the daytime, and *Komban-wa!* for the evening. As everyday phrases, there are many variations and contractions of these, formal and informal, and they differ between regions of Japan—but these are the universal standards!

Haven't seen you around for a while.

Hisashiburi.
久^{ひさ}しぶり。
Hisashiburi-dayone.
久^{ひさ}しぶりだよね。

This is the first of many overused phrases you'll come across in this book; *Hisashiburi* is a natural and integral part of a greeting to someone you haven't seen for a while.

How are you?

Genki?
元気^{げんき}？

How's it going?

Genki datta?
元気^{げんき}だった？
Saikin dō?　Genki?
最近^{さいきん}どう？　元気^{げんき}？

So we've met again.

Mata atta-ne.
また会^あったね。

I wanted to see you/   Aitakatta.
   I missed you.   会いたかった。

You can use this to a friend (as in "I missed you") or to your lover (as in "I was lonely without you"), though naturally you'll put more feeling into the latter. It can also be used about a third person.

How have you been   (Saikin) Dō-shiteta?
   doing (recently)?   （最近）どうしてた？
                              (Saikin) Nani-shiteta?
                              （最近）何してた？

What have you   Nani yatteta-no?
   been doing?   何やってたの？

Usually for asking what's happened just before or just recently (e.g. in the last week).

What's up?   Nanka kawatta-koto atta?
                  何か変わったことあった？

Not used as a first greeting, and more appropriate for someone you haven't seen for a while (e.g. a week, a month), especially if you think something might have changed. It literally means "Has something special (unusual) happened to you?" Answers could be *Betsu-ni* 別に, *Nani-mo* 何も ("Nothing much"), or a description of whatever has happened.

What's happening?　　　Dō-shita-no?
　　　　　　　　　　　　どうしたの？
You know what's going on, but you missed a bit of it.

　　　　　　　　　　　　Nanika atta-no?
　　　　　　　　　　　　<ruby>何<rt>なに</rt></ruby>かあったの？
For when you don't know what's going on.

What have you been　　Nani hanashiteta-no?
　　talking about?　　<ruby>何話<rt>なにはな</rt></ruby>してたの？

Nothing much.　　　　　Betsu-ni nani-mo.
　　　　　　　　　　　　<ruby>別<rt>べつ</rt></ruby>に<ruby>何<rt>なに</rt></ruby>も。
　　　　　　　　　　　　Betsu-ni.
　　　　　　　　　　　　<ruby>別<rt>べつ</rt></ruby>に。
　　　　　　　　　　　　Nani-mo.
　　　　　　　　　　　　<ruby>何<rt>なに</rt></ruby>も。
　　　　　　　　　　　　Tokuni (nai)
　　　　　　　　　　　　<ruby>特<rt>とく</rt></ruby>に（ない）。

Nothing special.　　　　Betsu-ni kawannai.
　　　　　　　　　　　　<ruby>別<rt>べつ</rt></ruby>に<ruby>変<rt>か</rt></ruby>わんない。
　　　　　　　　　　　　Aikawarazu.
　　　　　　　　　　　　<ruby>相変<rt>あいか</rt></ruby>わらず。

Okay, I guess.　　　　　Ammari.
　　　　　　　　　　　　あんまり。

I'm fine.　　　　　　　Genki.
　　　　　　　　　　　　<ruby>元気<rt>げんき</rt></ruby>。
　　　　　　　　　　　　Genki-yo. ♀
　　　　　　　　　　　　<ruby>元気<rt>げんき</rt></ruby>よ。
　　　　　　　　　　　　Genki-dayo. ♂
　　　　　　　　　　　　<ruby>元気<rt>げんき</rt></ruby>だよ。
　　　　　　　　　　　　Māne.
　　　　　　　　　　　　まあね。

So-so/Not good, not bad.   Mā-mā.
まあまあ。

What's wrong?   Dōka shita-no?
どうかしたの？
Nanka atta-no?
^{なん}何かあったの？

These are general enquiries about whether something is wrong, in a situation where you haven't noticed any particular problem.

Dō-shita-no?
どうしたの？

Asking this shows that you are much more sure (than with the above two phrases) that something is wrong, and so it should be voiced with more concern.

Dō-shitan-dayo? ♂
どうしたんだよ？

You ask this when there is clearly a problem, e.g. if the other person suddenly stops talking in the middle of a conversation.

I'm really busy   (Shigoto/Daigaku-de)
(with work/university).   taihen isogashii.
（^{し ごと}仕事・^{だいがく}大学で）^{たいへんいそが}大変忙しい。

I'm (a bit) sick.　　　　(Chotto) byōki-da.
（ちょっと）病気だ。

I've got a cold.　　　　Chotto kaze(-o) hiiteru.
ちょっと風邪をひいてる。

I'm (a bit) depressed.　　(Chotto) ochikonderu.
（ちょっと）落ちこ込んでる。

I'm tired.　　　　　　Tsukareteru/Tsukareta.
疲れてる・疲れた。

Tsukareteru is used in the general sense, whereas *Tsukareta* is more commonly used after an event or a hard day's work.

I'm sleepy.　　　　　Nemui.
眠い。

I'm not sleepy.　　　Nemukunai.
眠くない。

That's a bummer/tough!　Taihen-dane.
大変だね。
Taihen-dana. ♂
大変だな。

This is a classic Japanese expression of sympathy, disappointment, frustration. It's very flexible, and how you voice it adapts it to the situation. An understanding tone conveys sympathy with the other person's problems, or by adding force you show frustration with your own problems, which you can emphasise by making it *Taihen-dayo!* 大変だよ！

That can't be helped/　Shikata (-ga) nai-ne.
There's nothing you　仕方（が）ないね。
can do about it.

That's unfortunate/　Zannen-dane.
That's a shame.　残念だね。

Along with *Taihen,* these are more overworked phrases. *Shikata nai-ne* especially expresses a sense of helplessness—"A decision has been made higher up, and it's final." A sympathetic tone shows that you share the other person's feelings.

It'll be okay/It'll work out.   Nantoka naru-yo.
何とかなるよ。

Cheer up!   Genki dashite!
元気出して！
Genki dase-yo! ♂
元気出せよ！

These sorts of phrases will suffice for most greetings. The Japanese tend not to go into a lot of detail nor openly say what they think, especially in simple conversations, unless they're really excited or frustrated etc. Take your cues from those around you about how elaborate your explanations should be—as much as you can, fitting in is important!

What's on your mind?   Nani kangaeten-no?
何考えてんの？

Nothing.   Betsu-ni.
別に。
Nan-demo nai-yo.
何でもないよ。
Nani-mo.
何も。

Nan-demo nai-yo is a response to "What's wrong?" or "What's on your mind?" *Nani-mo* is a response to many questions, showing that there's nothing on your mind, that you don't want to say anything, or there's nothing happening.

I was just thinking.

Kangae-goto shiteta.
考えごとしてた。
Chotto.
ちょっと。

These answers show that you were thinking, but don't have anything to say about it.

Chotto-ne.
ちょっとね。

Chotto-ne shows that you were thinking, and invites the other person to ask about it.

I was just daydreaming.

Bōtto shiteta.
ぼーっとしてた。

Leave me alone!

Hottoite!
ほっといて！

It's none of your business!

Kankei nai-desho! ♀
関係ないでしょ！
Kankei nai-daro! ♂
関係ないだろう！
Yokei-na osewa!
よけいなお世話！

Is Sally okay?   Sarī genki?
                                      サリー元気？

How's Sally doing?   Sarī dō-shiteru?
                                      サリーどうしてる？

The answer to *Sarī genki?* will usually be "She's okay." and the
answer to *Sarī Dō-shiteru?* will usually be "She's okay. She has been
doing..." *Genki... shiteru* 元気…してる。 or "She's okay. She went
to..." *Genki... ni itta* 元気…に行った。 *Dō-shiteru?* should solicit a
longer answer.

Seen Jeff?   Jeffu minakatta?
                                      ジェフ見なかった？

I saw/met Kerry.   Kerii-ni atta.
                                      ケリーに会った。

I want to see you soon.   Sugu(-ni) aitai.
                                      すぐ（に）会いたい。

See you later.   Jā mata-ne.
                                      じゃあまたね。
                                      Mata-ne.
                                      またね。
                                      Mata.
                                      また。
                                      Bai-bai.
                                      バイバイ。

Goodbye.   Sayōnara.
                                      さようなら。

Yes and No 2

Yes.
    Hai.
    はい。
    Ee.
    ええ。
    Un.
    うん。

There are many ways to indicate agreement in Japanese, and these are the most direct. *Un* and *Uun* (see below) are very casual and natural, and they especially should be accompanied with gestures to make yourself clear.

No.
    Iie.
    いいえ。
    Uun.
    ううん。
    Iya,...
    いや、…

Iya is often used before another phrase, to explain or soften the disagreement, such as *iya, betsu-ni* いや、別に "no, not especially".

The Japanese, following their preference for indirectness, don't always say "yes" and "no" in the Western sense

That's right!
    ◆ Sō-dane!
      そうだね！
    ◆ Sō-dana! ♂
      そうだな！
    Mā-ne!
    まあね！

Mā-ne is often used to mean "I know." If said teasingly, it means "Yeah I know (but I might not tell you)." For example: "She's pretty, isn't she? Do you know her?" "Maybe I know her, maybe I don't." (*Mā-ne.*)

I think so too.

Sō omou.
そう思^もう。
Sō -yo-ne. ♀
そうよね。
◆ Sō -dayone.
そうだよね。

I agree (!)

Sansei (!)
賛成^{さんせい}（！）

So am I/Me too.

Watashi-mo. ♀
私^{わたし}も。
Boku-mo. ♂
僕^{ぼく}も。

**I see/I got it/
   I understand.**

Naruhodo.
なるほど。
Wakatta.
分^わかった。
Aa, sō-ka.
ああ、そうか。
Sokka.
そっか。
Sō, sō...
そう、そう…

Sō, sō... in particular is often used just to mean "I'm listening to you and understanding what you're saying." You'll soon pick up from the speech patterns of those around when they're questioning you with a variant of *so* and when they're just letting you know they're listening.

All right, that's OK.

Okkē.
オッケー。
Daijōbu(dayo).
大丈夫^{だいじょうぶ}（だよ）。

No problem.   Mondai nai-yo.
　　　　　　　　　 問題ないよ。

Colorful conversations can be created by injecting more than just a "yes" or "no." Study the following words and phrases. They can be voiced inquisitively or doubtfully, depending upon your tone of voice.

Really?   Hontō?
　　　　　　　 本当？

　　　　　　　 Hontō-ni?
　　　　　　　 本当に？

　　　　　　　 Maji-de?
　　　　　　　 まじで？

　　　　　　　 Maji?
　　　　　　　 まじ？

　　　　　　　 Uso/Ussō?
　　　　　　　 うそ？うっそー？

Is that so?   Sō-nano?
　　　　　　　　 そうなの？
　　　　　　　　 Sō?
　　　　　　　　 そう？

This has to be the most overused phrase in Japanese! Again, sometimes it just means "I'm listening to you" and sometimes it's used to ask for clarification etc. Non-verbal cues will tell you!

Did you/Do you/ Are you?	Sō-nano? そうなの？
Yeah, I know (groaned).	Sō-nan-dayonē. そうなんだよねえ。

For example: "Your car is no good!" *Kono kuruma wa dame*!
この車はだめ！ "Yeah, I know." *Sō-nan-dayonē.*

He/She/It seemed like one/that.	Sō mieta-yo. そう見えたよ。
I guess so.	Sō-dato omou. そうだと思う。 Sō-dane. そうだね。
It might be true.	◆ Sō -kamo-ne. そうかもね。
Maybe.	Tabun-ne. 多分ね。
Maybe not.	Chigaun-ja nai-(no). 違うんじゃない（の）。
That's not right.	Sonna-koto nai-yo. そんな事ないよ。
I wonder...	Sō-kanā... そうかなあ…
I don't think so/ I doubt it.	Sō omowanai. そう思わない。
I'm not sure.	Yoku wakaranai. よく分からない。

There's no way of knowing.	Wakaru-wake nai-yo. 分かる訳ないよ。

I can't say for sure.	Nanto-mo ienai. 何とも言えない。 Hakkiri ienai. はっきり言えない。

Because...	Datte... だって…

Datte is usually followed by an explanation.

But...	Demo... でも…

Usually followed by an explanation or a contradiction, such as "but, that's wrong." *Demo chigau-yo* でも、違うよ。

Here are some handy phrases for when you want to put questions back to the other speaker.

How come?	Nande? 何で？ Dō-shite? どうして？ Dō-shite-dayo? どうしてだよ？

What do you mean?　　　Dō-iu imi?
　　　　　　　　　　　　　どういう意味？

Is something wrong/　　　Kanji-ga chigau-yone.
　　different?　　　　　　感じが違うよね。
　　　　　　　　　　　　　Kanji-ga chigaun-dakedo.
　　　　　　　　　　　　　感じが違うんだけど。

You can ask this when the other person seems a bit different (e.g. from the last time you saw them).

　　　　　　　　　　　　　(Anoko,) Nan-ka chigawanai?
　　　　　　　　　　　　　（あの子、）何か違わない？

This is useful when a third person seems a bit different. *Anoko* means "That (young) person over there."

　　　　　　　　　　　　　Nan-ka chigau-no?
　　　　　　　　　　　　　何か違うの？

This is more suited to asking about things, not people.

What's the difference?　　Dō chigau-no?
　　　　　　　　　　　　　どう違うの？

What?　　　　　　　　　Nani?
　　　　　　　　　　　　　何？
　　　　　　　　　　　　　E?
　　　　　　　　　　　　　え？

Why not?　　　　　　　Nande (dame-nano)?
　　　　　　　　　　　　　何で（だめなの）？
　　　　　　　　　　　　　Nande dame-nan-dayo? ♂
　　　　　　　　　　　　　何でだめなんだよ？

Are you serious?　　　　Honki?
　　　　　　　　　　　　　本気？

Are you sure?

Hontō-ni?
本当に？

Zettai?
絶対？

Zettai? is a much more emphatic way to ask. *Hontō-ni?* is a safer bet in most situations. Clip the final *ni* for more emphasis.

You don't mean it?

Jōdan desho?
冗談でしょ？

(You're joking?)

Jōdan darō? ♂
冗談だろう？

But, of course, there are times when you want to make your point forcefully. Here are some words and phrases that will help you make a bigger impact. Just be careful with the negative ones!

Absolutely!

Zettai!
絶対！

Definitely!

Hontō-ni!
本当に！

Hontō-ni sō-dayone!
本当にそうだよね！

Hontō-ni sō-dayona! ♂
本当にそうだよな！

Majide.
まじで。

When using *Majide* to mean "Definitely," you can lengthen the final e sound, but don't raise the intonation (as with "Really?")

Of course!

Atarimae-deshō!
当たり前でしょう！

Atarimae-dayo! ♂
当たり前だよ！

Used in the sense of "That goes without saying!"

Mochiron!
もちろん！

Usually used as an answer to a question.

You better believe it!

Hontō-datte!
本当だって！
Hontō-dayo!
本当だよ！

That's it!

Sō-yo!
そうよ！
Sore-yo! ♀
それよ！
Sore-dayo! ♂
それだよ！

These phrases point out the best choice among (tangible or intangible) alternatives, e.g. after a question like "Which one?" *dore?* どれ？

That was good.

◆ Yokatta (yo)-ne.
よかった(よ)ね。

Right on! (Great!)
I did it!

Yatta!
やった！
Yosh! ♂
よし！
Ii-zo! ♂
いいぞ！

You're kidding me!	Karakawanai-de! からかわないで！ Uso-bakkari! うそばっかり！ Uso-bakka! うそばっか！

These phrases are commonly used by the Japanese, so don't confuse *bakka* (a short form of *bakkari* meaning "only" or "just") with *baka* ばか ("fool," an especially harsh insult in Osaka). For more emphasis, you could lengthen the last syllable or the *kk* pause of *bakkari*, or clip the last syllable of *bakka*.

This is too good to be true!	Uso-mitai! うそみたい！
No way/Stop joking! (a strong refusal)	Jōdan-ja nai-wayo! ♀ 冗談じゃないわよ！ Jōdan-ja nē-yo! ♂ 冗談じゃねえよ！
That's wrong!	Chigau-wayo! ♀ 違うわよ！ Chigau-yo! ♂ 違うよ！
That's impossible!	Dō-shiyō-mo nai-wayo! ♀ どうしようもないわよ！ Dō-shiyō-mo nai-yo! どうしようもないよ！ Shikata-ga nai-yo! 仕方がないよ！ Muri! むり！ Muri-yo! ♀ むりよ！ Muri-dane! ♂ むりだね！

Forget it!
   (I've had enough!)

Mō ii-yo!
もういいよ！

Bullshit!

Yoku iu-yo!
よく言うよ！

Literally means "How dare you say that!"

I don't care.
   (Anything's fine.)

Dō-demo ii-yo.
どうでもいいよ。
Kamawanai.
かまわない。

It means nothing to me.

Kankei nai-wa. ♀
関係ないわ。
Kankei nai-yo.
関係ないよ。

I'm not interested.

Kyōmi nai-wa. ♂
興味ないわ。
Kyōmi nai-yo.
興味ないよ。

Got a Minute?

Got a minute?

Jikan aru?
時間ある？
Chotto ii?
ちょっといい？

Till when?

Itsu-made?
いつまで？

(About) when?

Itsu-(goro)?
いつ（ごろ）？
Itsu-(gurai)?
いつ（ぐらい）？

About what time?

Nanji-goro?
何時ごろ？

Is it too early?

Haya-sugiru?
早過ぎる？

Is it too late?   Mō osoi?
　　　　　　　　もう遅い？

This "too late" refers to events in the past or now, e.g. *Eiga-o mini iku?* ("Shall we go see the movie) *Aa, mo osoi* 映画を見に行く？ [now]?" "Oh, it's too late." because it's already started.

　　　　　　　　Oso-sugiru?
　　　　　　　　遅すぎる？

This "too late" refers to events in the future, e.g. "Shall we go to the 11 o'clock movie?" *Jū-ichiji kara eiga- o miyō?* 11 時から映画を見よう。 *Aa, (owari wa) oso-sugiru* ああ、（終わりは）　遅過ぎる "Oh, it'll end too late." [because the trains will have stopped running so we can't get home etc.])

When is it convenient   Itsu-ga ii?
for you?   いつがいい？

How about the   Jūhachinichi-wa dō?
18th?   18 日はどう？

Then when can you   Itsu-nara ii?
make it?   いつならいい？
                        Itsu aiteru?
                        いつ空いてる？

You have already said *Itsu-ga ii?* and maybe even *Jūhachinichi-wa?* and they still can't decide.

What time can I come   Nanji-ni kureba ii?
over?   何時に来ればいい？

What time do we leave?   Nanji-ni iku?
                             何時に行く？
                             Nanji-ni deru?
                             何時に出る？

What time do we arrive?   Nanji-ni tsuku?
何時に着く？

The Japanese reputation for punctuality is well-earned. Suffice to say that if you make a promise to do something, especially as most people take public transport and have to plan accordingly, you should stick to your word! Dependability is highly valued in Japan, so if you can't make it on time, get in touch via mobile phone (see ON THE PHONE).

Are you ready?   Yōi dekita?
用意できた？
Mada?
まだ？
Ii?
いい？

When will you do it?   Itsu suru?
いつする？
Itsu yaru-no?
いつやるの？

How long will it take?   Dono-gurai kakaru?
どのぐらいかかる？

Next time. ◆ Kondo-ne.
今度ね。

Maybe later. Tabun kondo.
多分今度。

You will do it, but you don't know/haven't decided when.

Later. Ato-de.
後で。

You'll do it a few hours or so later.

◆ Sonouchi-ni-ne.
そのうちにね。

You'll do it a few days or weeks later. Alternatively, you may not want to do it and are fobbing someone off—this is a vague expression.

Soon. Mō-sugu.
もうすぐ。

Not yet. Mada.
まだ。

Not now. Ima-ja nakute.
今じゃなくて。

The last time Kono mae.
(you did something). この前。
Kono aida.
この間。
Konaida.
こないだ。

I don't know when. Itsu-(da)ka wakaranai.
いつ（だ）か分からない。

I don't know now. Ima chotto wakaranai.
今ちょっと分からない

I don't know yet.	Mada (chotto) wakaranai. まだ（ちょっと）分からない
Someday.	Itsu-ka. いつか。
Not next time.	Kondo-ja nai. 今度じゃない。 Kondo-ja naku. 今度じゃなく。
Anytime is fine.	Itsu-demo ii-yo. いつでもいいよ。
Always.	Itsumo. いつも。
You decide when.	Itsu-ka kimete. いつか決めて。 Jā kimete. じゃあ、決めて。
That's a bad day for me.	Sono hi (wa chotto) dame. その日（はちょっと）だめ。
That day is fine.	Jā sono hi-ne. じゃあ、その日ね。 Iiyo! いいよ！

Iiyo! said positively means "That's fine!" Don't say it negatively or glumly, or it'll mean "I've had enough" (see YES AND NO).

Let's begin!	Hajime-yō! 始めよう！ Jā yarō! じゃあ、やろう！

It'll only take a minute.   Sugu-dakara.
すぐだから。

Let's continue.   Tsuzuke-yō!
続けよう！

Do it later.   Ato-de shite.
後でして。

I'll be finished soon.   Sugu owaru.
すぐ終わる。

I've finished.   Owatta.
終わった。
Dekita.
できた。

Both of these are very common phrases, but *Dekita* only applies to something that has a clear start and finish, such as cooking dinner, a project or homework, but not work, which carries on the next day, and so isn't "finished" in the same sense. *Owatta* can apply to anything, including work. The limitation to *Dekita* also applies below.

Finished?   Owatta?
終わった？
Dekita?
できた？

Finished already?   Mō owatta?
もう終わった？
Mō dekita?
もうできた？

Say What? 4

Listen.

Kiite.
聞いて。

Listen to me.

Chotto kiite.
ちょっと聞いて。
Kiite-yo.
聞いてよ。

Don't listen/
　Don't ask me (that).

Kikanai-de.
聞かないで
Kikuna-yo. ♂
聞くなよ

Did you hear me/
　him/them?

Kikoeta?
聞こえた？

I couldn't hear.

Kikoenakatta.
聞こえなかった。

I didn't hear.

Kikanakatta.
聞かなかった。

I don't want to hear.

Kikitakunai.
聞きたくない。

Speak up.

Motto ōkii-koe-de hanashite.
もっと大きい声で話して。

Speak more slowly.

Motto yukkuri itte.
もっとゆっくり言って。

Say it again.　　　　　　　　Mō ikkai itte.
　　　　　　　　　　　　　　もう1回言って。
　　　　　　　　　　　　　　Mō ichido itte.
　　　　　　　　　　　　　　もう1度言って。

With sentences such as these, which are essentially requests often voiced as statements, it's softer to use a rising intonation and/or add *kureru*? くれる？ to the end of the sentence. If you use a falling intonation the request is harsher, more like an order. Women especially should use this with care.

Let's talk in Japanese.　　　Nihongo(-de) hanasō.
　　　　　　　　　　　　　　日本語(で)話そう。

Let's talk in English.　　　　Eigo(-de) hanasō.
　　　　　　　　　　　　　　英語(で)話そう。

It's a cliché, but the Japanese are generally ashamed of their English-speaking ability. The Japanese school system teaches them very precise and technical grammar, but not how to speak. Even those who go to *Eikaiwa* 英会話 (private English conversation schools) aren't very good, or confident even if they are. A sure-fire way to get the conversation bubbling is to use the following two stock phrases.

You're good at English.　　　Eigo jōzu-(da)ne.
　　　　　　　　　　　　　　英語上手(だ)ね。
　　　　　　　　　　　　　　Eigo umai-ne.
　　　　　　　　　　　　　　英語うまいね。

This will usually be followed by an embarrassed denial. To show that you really mean it, say...

Yes, you really are good.	Un, jōzu-dayo.
	うん、上手だよ。
	Un, umai-yo.
	うん、うまいよ。

Even if you carry on in Japanese, you'll have made a good impression!

Where did you learn/ are you learning English?	Doko-de eigo-o benkyo shita/ shiteru-no?
	どこで英語を勉強した／してるの？

How long did you learn/ have you been learning English for?	Dono-gurai eigo-o benkyo shita/ shiteru-no?
	どのぐらい英語を勉強した／ してるの？

To prolong the topic of conversation, and to make a Japanese person feel really good about his/her English, you can ask if he/she has been overseas.

Have you studied English overseas/in America/ in the UK?	Gaikoku/Amerika/Igirisu-de (eigo-o) benkyo shita koto aru?
	外国／アメリカ／イギリスで （英語を）勉強したことある？

If they have, and elaborate a little, you can say "That's great" *sugoi-ne* 凄いね. If they haven't, the classic ingratiating reply is to express surprise and reiterate that their English is fantastic.

But your English is so good!	Demo, eigo (sugoku) jōzu-ne. ♀
	でも、英語（すごく）上手ね。
	Demo, eigo (sugoku) umai-ne.
	英語（すごく）うまいね。

By the way, a foreigner who speaks even a little Japanese will be constantly praised in ways like this. This is just one reason it's good to make an effort!

Say something.	Nanka itte.
	何か言って。

What are you talking about?	Nani ni-tsuite hanashiteru-no? 何について話してるの？ Nani itten-no? 何言ってんの？ Nani itten-dayo? ♀ 何言ってんだよ？

The last two are more accusative, and are especially used when you want to oppose or criticise the speaker.

Let's keep talking about it.	Hanashi-o-tsuzuke-yō. 話を続けよう。 Motto hanasō. もっと話そう。
Let's talk about it later.	(Sore-wa) ato-de hanasō. （それは）後で話そう。
I don't want to talk.	Hanashitakunai. 話したくない。
I don't want to talk about it.	Sore ni tsuite hanashitakunai. それについて話したくない。 Mō sono-koto wa hanashitakunai. もうそのことは話したくない。
By the way...	Tokoro-de... ところで...
Just to change the subject...	Chotto hanashi-ga kawaru kedo... ちょっと話が変わるけど...

Before the conversation is about to zoom off into the realms of unpleasantness, there are a few ways you can try to lighten the mood. A good one is the "crazy foreigner" routine. The Japanese are fond of onomatopoeias, words that imitate sounds, and used at the right moment, the following will produce a laugh or three.

dog barking	wan-wan ワンワン
cat meowing	nyan-nyan ニャンニャン
light rain	shito-shito シトシト para-para パラパラ
heavy rain	za-za ザーザー
light crying	shiku-shiku シクシク

Rub your eyes while saying *shiku-shiku*.

heavy crying	en-en エンエン
walking noise	teku-teku テクテク
(beer) drinking noise	goku-goku ゴクゴク
sucking noise	sū-sū スースー
I'm hungry.	Onaka-ga peko-peko. おなかがペコペコ
My head feels dizzy.	Atama-ga fura-fura. 頭がフラフラ。

I have a sharp pain in my stomach.

I-ga kiri-kiri itai.
胃がキリキリ痛い。

But then again, sometimes even the best comics have to put their foot down...

Don't make excuses.

Iiwake shinai-de.
言い訳しないで。

That's not a good excuse.

Sore iiwake janai!
それ言い訳じゃない！

Stop complaining!

Butsu butsu iwanaide! ♀
ブツブツ言わないで！
Butsu butsu iu-na! ♂
ブツブツ言うな！
Monku bakka(ri) iu-nayo! ♂
文句ばっか（り）言うなよ！

Do you know what you're saying?

Nani itten- no?
何言ってんの？

This, voiced with incredulity, implies that the other person is saying crazy things.

Nani itten-daka wakatten-no?
何言ってんだか分かってんの？

This is harsh! It's a sure bet to enrage the other person. If they are talking rubbish it'll put them in their place, but be careful!

You said that, didn't you?   Sō itte-takke?
そう言ってたっけ？
Sō itta-yone?
そう言ったよね？
Sō itetta-deshō? ♀
そう言ってたでしょう？
So itteta-darō? ♂
そう言ってただろう？

Sō itte-takke? means "I don't remember, but I think you said that, right?" It can also be used about yourself, such as "Oh, did I say that?" It and *So itta-yone?* are part "I don't remember..." and part accusative, and pronunciation will show the difference. The last two are outright accusative, and should be used with caution.

I didn't say anything.   Nani-mo ittenai-yo.
何も言ってないよ。

This sentence is in the general sense, such as in response to "Did you spread the latest rumor?"

Nani-mo iwana-katta.
何も言わなかった。

This sentence should be used about a particular subject and/or communication to one person, such as "Did you tell her my secret?"

You'd better not say things like that.   Sonna-koto iwanai-hō ga ii-ne.
そんな事言わない方がいいね。
Sonna-koto iccha-dame-yo. ♀
そんな事言っちゃだめよ。
Sonna-koto iccha-dame-dayo. ♂
そんな事言っちゃだめだよ。

The last two sentences are quite harsh, sitting close to the following in forcefulness.

Don't say things like that.   Sonna-koto iu-na-yo. ♂
そんな事言うなよ。

Don't talk so loudly.
Sonna-ni-ōkii-koe-de shaberanaide/
hanasanaide.
そんなに大きい声でしゃべら
ないで／話さないで。

Comings and Goings 5

Come here.	Chotto kite. ちょっと来て。
Come over.	Oide-yo. おいでよ。
Come later.	Ato-de kite. 後で来て。
Can you come?	Koreru? 来れる？
Won't you come with us/me?	Issho-ni konai/kuru? 一緒に来ない／来る？
She/He is coming here.	Kanojo/kare kuru-yo. 彼女／彼来るよ。
I'm coming, wait a second.	Ima iku. 今行く。
I can go.	Ikeru. 行ける。
I think I can go.	Ikeru-to omou-yo. 行けると思うよ。
I can't go.	Ikenai. 行けない。
I want to go.	Ikitai. 行きたい。

I want to go to Tokyo.   Tōkyō(-e/ni)-ikitai.
東京（へ／に）行きたい。

I really want to go.   Hontō-ni ikitai.
本当に行きたい。
Chō-ikitai.
チョー行きたい。

I don't want to go.   Ikitakunai.
行きたくない。

I really don't want to go.   Hontō-ni ikitakunai.
本当に行きたくない。

You went, didn't you?   Itta-deshō?
行ったでしょう？
Itta-yo-nē?
行ったよねえ？
Itta-yo-nā? ♂
行ったよなあ？
Ittan-deshō? ♀
行ったんでしょう？
Ittan-dayo-nē?
行ったんだよねえ？

The last two phrases are more positive, as in "I know you went
(because she told me)!"

I went.   Itta.
行った

I didn't go.   Ikanakatta.
行かなかった。

Don't go.   Ikanaide.
行かないで。
Ikuna-yo. ♂
行くなよ。

Don't go yet.	Mada ikanaide.
	まだ行かないで。
	Mada ikuna-yo. ♂
	まだ行くなよ。
I must go now.	Ikanakucha.
	行かなくちゃ。
May I go?	Itte-mo-ii?
	行ってもいい？
Shall we go?	Iku?
	行く？
Let's go.	Ikō.
	行こう。
	Sā, ikuka.
	さあ、行くか。
	Mō ikō.
	もう行こう。

Mō ikō is said if you should leave because of the time, as in "We should go now or we'll be late."

Let's leave/get out of here.	Mō deyō.
	もう出よう。

Said only when inside a building, car etc.

I'm leaving soon.	Mō sugu deru.
	もうすぐ出る。
She/He has left here.	Kanojo/kare icchatta-yo.
	彼女／彼行っちゃったよ。
She/He has gone home.	Kanojo/kare kaecchatta-yo.
	彼女／彼帰っちゃったよ。
Stay here.	Koko-ni ite.
	ここにいて。

Where are you going?　　Doko iku-no?
　　　　　　　　　　　　どこ行くの？

Please go first/After you.　Osaki-ni dōzo.
　　　　　　　　　　　　お先にどうぞ。
　　　　　　　　　　　　Saki-ni dōzo.
　　　　　　　　　　　　先にどうぞ。

Thanks for letting me　　Saki-ni gomen-ne.
go first.　　　　　　　先にごめんね。

Take your time　　　　Yukkuri itte.
(go slowly).　　　　　ゆっくり行って。

I'm lost.　　　　　　　Michi-ni mayotta.
　　　　　　　　　　　　道に迷った。

This is used when you've lost your way.

　　　　　　　　　　　　Wakaranai.
　　　　　　　　　　　　分からない。

This is used when you don't understand.

Please tell me the way.　Iki-kata-o oshiete-kureru?
　　　　　　　　　　　　行き方を教えてくれる？

Could you write it down?　Kaite-kureru?
　　　　　　　　　　　　書いてくれる？

There are many transport options in Japan, but (for most purposes) the trains (*densha* 電車) are by far the best. They are clean, air-conditioned and impeccably punctual, so you can plan your itinerary to the minute if you want! There are lines serving almost all parts of the country, with the famous *Shinkansen* (新幹線 bullet trains) for fast inter-city trips, subways (*chikatetsu* 地下鉄) criss-crossing the cities and regular trains in between. Trains, especially the *Shinkansen* and *tokkyu* (特急 limited expresses) can often be quite expensive, but for ultra-reliable mass transportation they can't be beaten.

Buses (*basu* バス) are good for short trips around town and the suburbs, but the traffic congestion hampers their reliability. Highway buses (*haiuēbasu* ハイウェーバス) are a cheap way to get between major cities, many running overnight, but again, crowded roads mean that the timetables are a rough guide only. Planes (*hikōki* 飛行機) are a good choice for inter-island (especially to Hokkaidō, where there is no *Shinkansen*) and long-distance travel, but prices vary (train prices are constant) so it pays to book early.

And like many things, cars (*kuruma* 車) are expensive in Japan, with a myriad of taxes and laws adding cost and hassle. Unless you're living in an isolated area, it's much easier to get around on public transport. The system can be daunting, but the ticket vending machines are all essentially the same and all signs are written in *romaji,* so once mastered, it's easy. Here are some key phrases to help you ask the way.

Don't forget (to tell me) the train station names.	Eki-mei o wasurenaide. 駅名を忘れないで。
Which train/bus should I take?	Docchi-no densha/basu-nano? どっちの電車／バスなの？
Where do I get off?	Doko-de oriru-no? どこで降りるの？

Get off at ... (station/ bus stop).

...eki/basutei-de orite.

... 駅／バス停で降りて。

Eki ("station") is added to the proper name of some stations, but not to all e.g. *Kyōto-eki* 京都駅, *Hanshin Umeda* 阪神梅田, etc.

How will I know when to get off?

Itsu oriru-ka dō wakaru-no?

いつ降りるかどう分かるの？

(It's OK), you'll hear the station name on the PA.

Anaunsu-de ekimei-ga nagareru. (Daijōbu-dayo).

アナウンスで駅名が流れる。 （大丈夫だよ）。

(About) how much does it cost?

Ikura (gurai) kakaru-no?

いくら（ぐらい）かかるの？

I'll be waiting at the ticket gate/the station office/by the ticket machines/in front of the station/at the bus stop.

Kaisatsuguchi/ekiinshitsu/ kippu-uriba/ekimae/ basutei-de matteru.

改札口／駅員室／切符売り場／ 駅前／バス停で待ってる。

Eat, Drink, Be Merry

6

Eating and drinking are vital parts of socializing in Japan. With relations at work often quite hierarchical and stiff, going out and relaxing becomes very important to relieve stress and tension. Even within a relaxed university environment, people still enjoy the liveliness of alcohol and food-fueled conversation.

There are many special occasions when the Japanese will eat out or have a big meal in. Apart from birthdays, family occasions like after students' graduations (from every school) and the *seijinshiki* 成人式 (coming-of-age ceremony at age 20, held on the second Monday in January), and work-centered events like *hanami* 花見 ("flower viewing" or drinks under the cherry trees in March/April) are ideal times to get together over some food and drink.

For a description of going out options, see CHECK IT OUT, and for ways to chat up the opposite sex, see CHITCHAT. For strictly food-related phrases, read on.

I'm hungry.	Onaka(-ga) suita. おなか (が) すいた。 Hara hetta. ♂ 腹へった。
I'd like to eat something.	Nanka tabetai. 何か食べたい。
I haven't eaten yet.	Mada tabetenai. まだ食べてない。
Do you want to eat?	Tabetai? 食べたい？

I don't want to eat.

Tabetakunai.
食べたくない。

I won't eat.

Tabenai.
食べない。

Did you eat lunch/dinner?

Gohan tabeta?
ご飯食べた？

What would you like?

Nani-ga hoshii?
何が欲しい？

Used more in a shopping context.

Nani-ga ii?
何がいい？

Best suited to eating contexts.

What's that?

Nani sore?
何それ？

Not that.

Sore-ja nakute.
それじゃなくて。

Do you want to eat some more?

Motto taberu?
もっと食べる？

I'm thirsty.

Nodo(-ga) kawaita.
のど（が）乾いた。

**I'd like a beer/wine/
chūhai.**

Bīru/wain/chūhai(-ga) nomitai.
ビール／ワイン／チューハイ（が）
飲みたい。

Chūhai are alcoholic drinks based on *shōchū,* a kind of Japanese vodka. They come in at about 5%, in sweet and sour flavors and are easy to drink—but bite hard the next day! To avoid hangovers (*futsukayoi* 二日酔い) you could settle for the following.

**I'd like a soft drink/cola/
melon soda/juice/
coffee/tea/green tea.**

Sofuto dorinku/kōra/meron sōda
jūsu/kōhī/kōcha/ocha(-ga)
nomitai.
ソフトドリンク／コーラ／
メロン・ソーダ／ジュース／
コーヒー／紅茶／お茶が飲み
たい。

I don't want to drink.

Nomitakunai.
飲みたくない。

I won't drink.

Nomanai.
飲まない。

I haven't drunk yet.

Mada nondenai.
まだ飲んでない。

**Do you want to drink
something?**

Nanka nomu?
何か飲む？

**Do you want to drink
some more?**

Motto nomu?
もっと飲む？

**Thank you, but I still
have some.**

Arigatō, demo mada aru-kara.
ありがとう、でもまだあるから。

Drink a little bit more.
Mō-sukoshi non-de.
もう少し飲んで。
Mō-chotto non-de.
もうちょっと飲んで。
Mō-choi non-de.
もうちょい飲んで。

How about (some) dinner?
Shokuji shinai?
食事しない？
Gohan taberu?
ご飯食べる？

Note that when talking about meals, *gohan* (literally "rice") is more commonly used in informal situations than *shokuji* (literally "meal").

Is the meal ready?
Shokuji dekita?
食事できた？
Gohan mada?
ご飯まだ？

It's ready.
Dekita.
できた。

Have you ordered?
Chūmon shita?
注文した？
Tanonda?
頼んだ？

When visiting someone's house/eating a meal they've cooked, respect for the food (and hence their feelings) is the watchword! There is a huge array of unusual (to Western eyes) food in Japan, and you sometimes get the feeling that your hostess will cook a few particularly unusual things for you to try. You're generally not expected to like everything, but you must try things—such an adventurous spirit is admired in Japan!

Will you try this (food)?
Tabete miru?
食べてみる？

Try this!   (Kore) tabete mite.
                                       （これ）食べてみて。

What's it called?   Nante iu-no?
                                       何て言うの？

I've never tried...   ...tabeta kotonai.
                                       ...食べたことない。

Even if you've been in Japan for a while and your hosts know that,
expect to be asked what your favorite Japanese food is, and
whether or not you can eat the more challenging varieties. It's just
something you have to get used to as a stepping stone to more
interesting food-related conversation.

What's your favorite   Nihon-no tabemono-no naka-de,
Japanese food?   dore-ga ichiban suki?
                                       日本の食べ物の中で、どれが
                                          一番好き？

Can you eat *nattō/anko*?   Nattō/anko taberareru?
                                       納豆／あんこ食べられる？

Nattō is fermented soybeans, which are stringy and foul-smelling.
Anko is the general name for sweet soybean paste, and like *nattō* is
often unpalatable to foreigners, hence the Japanese often asking if
you can eat them.

Yes, I can.   Un, taberareru(-yo).
                                       うん、食べられる（よ）。

No, I can't.   Uun, taberarenai.
                                       ううん、食べられない。

There is no shame whatsoever in saying this! Of course, you could
also say that you've never tried it *Tabetemita koto ga nai* 食べてみた
ことがない。 But that might prompt your hosts to offer you some!

(That) looks delicious.	(Are) oishisō. （あれ）おいしそう。
It smells good.	Ii kaori. いい香り。
Give me a bit more.	Mō sukoshi. もう少し。 Mō chotto. もうちょっと。
Gimme more.	(Motto) chōdai. もっとちょうだい。
Enough.	Jūbun. 充分。 Tariru. 足りる。
Enough?	Tarita? 足りた？
Not enough.	Tarinai. 足りない。
(Sorry,) I can't eat that.	(Sumimasen,) Sore tabe(ra)renai. （すみません）それ食べ（ら） れない。
Itadakimas!	Itadakimas! いただきます！

Almost every Japanese says this before eating, in almost any situation. The closest English equivalent is "grace," but it has lost its religious meaning (of receiving from the gods). Don't hesitate to say this before a meal, and you may even be complimented on your good manners!

Does this taste good?   Kore oishii?
                              これおいしい？

It tastes good.   Oishii (!)
                              おいしい（！）

This is another grossly overworked word, which can be voiced with the full gamut of emotions, from excited enthusiasm to indifference (meaning that it may not be good at all!). The Japanese tend not to be specific about what they think of the texture or flavor—they just show how they feel about it by how much emotion they put into saying *oishii*. You can add other words, such as *kekkō oishii* 結構おいしい ("It's really good" even without much enthusiasm), but just saying *oishii* and meaning it is usually enough.

It's an unusual taste.   Fushigi-na aji-dane.
                              不思議な味だね。

It's okay/So-so.   Mā-mā.
                              まあまあ。

These two are also polite ways of saying you don't really like something, especially if it's something the other person has made. (If they're really proud of it, it's best to say *oishii* but be less enthusiastic than normal). The following three phrases are also handy, but best left for eating out, where you won't be insulting anyone by criticizing the food!

It's not good.   Yokunai.
                              よくない。

It doesn't taste good.　　　Oishikunai.
　　　　　　　　　　　　　　おいしくない。

It's awful.　　　　　　　Mazui.
　　　　　　　　　　　　　　まずい。
　　　　　　　　　　　　　　Hidoi.
　　　　　　　　　　　　　　ひどい。

I'm full.　　　　　　　　Onaka(-ga) ippai.
　　　　　　　　　　　　　　お腹(が)いっぱい。

Gochisosama(-deshita)!　　Gochisosama(-deshita)!
　　　　　　　　　　　　　　ごちそうさま(でした)！

This is the end-of-meal counterpart to *itadakimas*. It literally means "It was a feast," and is a sign of appreciation.

The Way I Feel

7

I like it.

Suki.
好き。
Suki-dayo.
好きだよ。

I like it a lot.

Daisuki.
大好き。
Daisuki-dayo.
大好きだよ。

I love it!

Meccha-meccha suki!
メッチャメッチャ好き！

Meccha is an Ōsaka slang word meaning "very" that has caught on nationwide.

It's OK/so-so.

Mā-mā.
まあまあ。

I don't like it very much.

Anmari suki-ja nai.
あんまり好きじゃない。

If someone is offering you something but you really don't want it, say this to avoid hurting their feelings. *Mā-mā* is a politer way of saying this.

I hate it.

Suki janai.
好きじゃない。
Kirai.
嫌い。
Kirai-dayo.
嫌いだよ。

I hate it a lot.　　　　　Daikirai.
　　　　　　　　　　　　　大嫌い。
　　　　　　　　　　　　　Daikirai-dayo.
　　　　　　　　　　　　　大嫌いだよ。

I really hate it.　　　　Hontō-ni/Maji-de kirai.
　　　　　　　　　　　　　本当に／まじで嫌い。

The Japanese tend not be too open about what they don't like.
Using anything below *suki janai* is really firing off verbal bullets—
pick your target carefully!

I want...(object).　　　...-ga hoshii.
　　　　　　　　　　　　　…が欲しい。

I really want...(object).　Chō/Hontō-ni/Maji-de
　　　　　　　　　　　　　　...-ga hoshii.
　　　　　　　　　　　　　チョー／本当に／まじで
　　　　　　　　　　　　　　…が欲しい。

I want...(action).　　　...-ga shitai.
　　　　　　　　　　　　　…がしたい。

I really want...(action).　Chō/Hontō-ni/Maji-de
　　　　　　　　　　　　　　... ga-shitai.
　　　　　　　　　　　　　チョー／本当に／まじで
　　　　　　　　　　　　　　…がしたい。

I don't want...(object).　Ii.
　　　　　　　　　　　　　いい。
　　　　　　　　　　　　　Iranai.
　　　　　　　　　　　　　いらない。
　　　　　　　　　　　　　Hoshikunai
　　　　　　　　　　　　　欲しくない。

I really don't want/　　Hontō-ni/maji-de iranai.
　　need...(object).　　本当に／まじでいらない。
　　　　　　　　　　　　　Hontō-ni/maji-de hoshikunai.
　　　　　　　　　　　　　本当に／まじで欲しくない。

I don't want…(action).	Iya.
	いや。
	Yada.
	やだ。
	Yada-yo.
	やだよ。

| **I really don't want…** | Hontō-ni/Maji-de… shitakunai. |
| **(action).** | 本当に／まじで…したくない。 |

The Japanese usually differentiate between wanting an object (noun) and wanting action (verb). The distinction isn't absolute—you will hear …*shitehoshii* …して欲しい ("I want to do…")—and it varies between speakers and regions, but we'll keep it simple here.

If you want an object (for example, chewing gum), place the noun in front of *ga hoshii*. E.g. *Gamu-ga hoshii* ガムが欲しい (I want some gum.) If you want an action (to go), add *tai* to the verb (stem form). E.g. *Ikitai* 行きたい (I want to go.)

The negative form works in much the same way, just changing the final *-i* to *-kunai*. E.g. *Gamu-ga hoshikunai* ガムが欲しくない (I don't want any gum.) Or, more commonly but less politely, you can just say *Iranai* いらない (I don't want/need [it]).

For not wanting an action, add *takunai* to the verb stem. E.g. *Ikitakunai* 行きたくない (I don't want to go), *shitakunai* (I don't want to do it), or you can just say *Iya*, *Yada*, or *Yada-yo* (I don't want [to]). Because these last three are already rough slang, they should not be said harshly, or their meaning would be too strong.

Ii is for either objects and actions, but can indicate wanting as well as not wanting something, depending on how it is voiced. A falling intonation and negative gestures means no, and with enthusiastic delivery plus positive gestures it means yes. This is a common word that needs great care!

| **I'm busy.** | Isogashii. |
| | 忙しい。 |

I'm happy.	Ureshii. (joyous) 嬉しい。 Shiawase. (fortunate) 幸せ。
I'm happy to hear that.	Sore kiite ureshii. それ聞いて嬉しい。
I'm glad to know that.	Sore kiite yokatta. それ聞いてよかった。
I'm sad.	Kanashii. 悲しい。
I'm fine.	Genki. 元気。
I'm mad/I'm mad at you!	Atama-ni-kita! 頭にきた！ Atama-kita! 頭きた！ Atama-kuru! 頭くる！

For these phrases, *atama* is pronounced differently than when said by itself. It should be said quickly, in a staccato manner, such as *ah-tah-mah-*... And usually these phrases are said jokingly; if you tell your wife that she's "silly," she'll definitely reply *Atama-kita*!

I'm ready.	Yōi dekita. 用意できた。
I'm tired.	Tsukareta. 疲れた。
I'm freaked.	Bibitta. びびった。

I'm surprised!   Odoroita!
                                  驚いた！
                                  Bikkuri shita!
                                  ビックリした！

Bikkuri shita is more common, and a more natural exclamation.

What a relief.   Hotto shita.
                                  ほっとした。
                                  Yokatta.
                                  良かった。

**I'm relieved (to hear   Anshin shita.
     that).**   安心した。

I'm scared.   Kowai.
                                  怖い。

**I feel sick. (That's   Kimochi warui.
   sickening/Yuck.**   気持ち悪い。

I'm disappointed.　　Gakkari shichatta.
ガッカリしちゃった。
Gakkari shita-yo.
ガッカリしたよ。

I was worried.　　Shimpai shita.
心配した。

I can do it.　　Dekiruyo.
できるよ。

Can you do it?　　Dekiru?
できる？

I can't do it.　　Dekinai.
できない。

Can't you do it?　　Dekinai-no?
できないの？

I can't help it/　　Shikata nai-yo.
That can't be helped.　仕方ないよ。
Shō-ga nai-yo.
しょうがないよ。

Sorry, I can't.　　Warui-kedo dame.
悪いけどだめ。
Warui-kedo dame-da.
悪いけどだめだ。

I should do it/ **I gotta do it.**	Shinakucha. しなくちゃ。 Yaranakucha. やらなくちゃ。
I'll do it.	Atashi-ga suru. ♀ あたしがする。 Atashi-ga yaru. ♀ あたしがやる。 Boku-ga suru. ♂ 僕がする。 Boku-ga yaru. ♂ 僕がやる。
I'm tired of it.	Mō akite kichatta. もう飽きてきちゃった。 Mō akita. もう飽きた。
I understand.	Wakatta. 分かった。
I understand very well.	Yoku wakatta. よく分かった。
I think I understand.	Wakatta-to omou. 分かったと思う。
I don't understand.	Wakaranai. 分からない。
I don't understand very **well.**	Yoku wakaranai. よく分からない。
I know.	Wakatteru. 分かってる。 Shitteru. 知ってる。

Wakatteru, which is used mostly for actions, means "Even if you didn't mention it, I knew that." Or "Okay, I'll do it, so stop your nagging!" E.g. "Go and clean your room." *Wakatteru.* (I know I need to do it.) "The party starts at 7 p.m." *Wakatteru.* (I know [because I already heard about it].) *Shitteru* can be used for objects and actions. E.g. "I know (her)" and "I know (how to get there)." *Shitteru.*

I know that person.	Ano hito shitteru. あの人知ってる。
Do you know that?	Sore shitteru? それ知ってる？
Ah, you know that.	Aa, shitten-da. ああ、知ってんだ。
I don't know.	Shiranai. 知らない。
I didn't know.	Shiranakatta. 知らなかった。
I didn't know that, though.	Shiranakatta-kedo. 知らなかったけど。
You know (knew) that, don't (didn't) you?	Shitteru/ta-deshō? 知ってる／たでしょう？

Give me time to think it over.	Kangae-sasete. 考えさせて。
I'll think about it.	Kangae-toku-yo. 考えとくよ。
I'm so confused.	Atama-ga kongaragatta. 頭がこんがらがった。 Nandaka yoku wakaranai. 何だかよく分からない。 Mō wakannai! もう分かんない！
I made a mistake.	Machigaeta. 間違えた。
I blew it.	Shippai shita. 失敗した。
Am I right?	Atteru? あってる？
Am I wrong?	Machigatteru? 間違ってる？

Atteru? and *Machigatteru?* are used to clarify whether or not what you've said or done was right.

What a pity!	Kawaisō! かわいそう！
Too bad.	Okinodoku. お気の毒。 ◆ Hidoi-ne. ひどいね。 ◆ Hidoi-na. ♂ ひどいな。

These may all be used in a sympathetic or sarcastic context, depending upon your tone of voice.

I hope so.	Sō-dato ii-ne. そうだといいね。
It's risky!	Yabai! やばい！
Go! Go for it! **(Good luck!)**	Gambatte! 頑張って！ Gambare! 頑張れ！

Gambare! is stronger, and is used in any situation (speaking directly to someone who is about to sit a test/play sport, cheering for your favorite team, encouraging runners in a marathon etc). *Gambatte* is usually only used when speaking directly to someone. When used before the event, these phrases are the normal Japanese equivalent to "good luck."

	Kintama doko-ni tsuiteru-no? ♂ 金玉どこに付いてるの？

This literally means "Where are your balls?" Guys can use this to other guys if they aren't trying very hard in a sports match or in picking up girls.

Calm down!	Ochitsuite! 落ち着いて！ Asenna-yo! ♂ あせんなよ！
Cheer up!	Genki dashite! ♀ (g→b) 元気出して！ Genki dase-yo! ♂ 元気出せよ！
Never mind.	Ki-ni shinai-de. 気にしないで。 Ki-ni sunna-yo. ♂ 気にすんなよ。

Cool.   Kakkoii.

かっこいい。

Said especially about boys and cars.

Uncool.   Dasai.

ダサい。

This is an abbreviation of *Datte, Saitama no...*   だって、埼玉の…
("But, that's from Saitama"), a phrase first used by downtown
Tokyo-ites, meaning that something comes from the unfashionable
outer suburb of Saitama.

Really cool.   Saikō.

最高。

Maji-de kakkoii.

まじでかっこいい。

Chō kakkoii.

チョーかっこいい。

Awesome.   Sugoi.

すごい。

Sugē. ♂

すげえ。

Cute.   Kawaii.

かわいい。

Kawaii is more commonly said by girls.

Really cute.   Chō kawaii.
チョーかわいい。
Sugoi kawaii.
すごいかわいい。

If there's one thing you must understand about the world of Japanese romance, it's the power of "cute," and in Japanese it has a much broader meaning than just small fluffy things. Say tennis is in fashion, but you don't know how to play. It's not really important because, come spring, like all style-conscious Japanese, you must carry a tennis racket everywhere. It's doesn't matter how well you play, what counts is that you have a cute cover for your racket, preferably with three Mickey Mouse patches and some English words. And the English should not make sense—something like "Active Sports: Traditional Mind for Specialty" would do nicely.

Clever/smart.   ◆ Atama ii-ne.
頭いいね。
◆ Kashikoi.
賢い。

Copycat.   Manekko.
まねっこ。

Ugly.   Kakko warui.
かっこ悪い。
Dasai.
ダサい。

Curses and Insults 8

The next two chapters are full of words to use when you're ready to get stuck into someone and tell them what you think! This chapter is general insults and tough talk that you can throw into conversations to add a bit of punch, and the next, STREET FIGHTING, is about some nasty situations you could end up in while in Japan—and ways out of them!

There are two things to bear in mind when ripping into someone with phrases like these. First, make sure they were insulting or trying to harm you! Sometimes the Japanese pay compliments in seemingly strange and roundabout ways. And secondly, if you do decide to unleash, make sure your attitude matches the words. Remember what we said about how you say things being as important as what you say? A forceful phrase said softly just sounds silly, but a punchy phrase backed with menace is frightening.

Damn it!   Chikushō!
                                ちくしょう！
Usually said to yourself.

Shit!   Kuso!
                                くそ！
Meaning "fæces," Kuso! can be said to yourself, just as Westerners say "Shit!"

Shit, I fucked up!   Ikkenai! ♀
   Oh, shit!   いっけない！
                                Ikkene! ♂
                                いっけね！
Literally means "It's not good!" Usually said to yourself.

What do you want?!

Nani-yo?! ♀
何よ？！
Nanda-yo! ♂
何だよ！
Nanka monku aru-no?
何か文句あるの？

These are basic, all-round good phrases to use when someone really pisses you off. They usually command respect, or at least let you establish yourself.

What did you say?

Nante itta-no?
何て言ったの？
Nante ittan-dayo? ♂
何て言ったんだよ？

Who do you think you're talking to?

Dare-ni mukatte itten-dayo? ♂
誰に向かって言ってんだよ？

Why do you talk like that?!

Nande sonna-koto iu-no?!
何でそんな事言うの？！
Nande sonna-koto iun-dayo?! ♂
何でそんな事言うんだよ？！

If you're positive a Japanese person is talking derogatorily about you, these phrases are good to use. But be careful, sometimes they're complimenting you!

Are you stupid, or what?   Baka-janai?

ばかじゃない？

This phrase is a superb example of the importance of pronunciation. To mean "Are you stupid, or what?" you must use a rising intonation (making it a rhetorical question). With a flat or falling intonation it means the opposite, "I'm/You're no fool!"

You're stupid!   Baka!

ばか！

Baka-yarō! ♂

ばかやろう！

You look stupid!   Baka-mitai!

ばかみたい！

That's stupid!   Baka-mitai!

ばかみたい！

Baka-jan!

ばかじゃん！

-Jan is a colloquial suffix which means the same as -deshō?/-darō? -でしょう？ -だろう？or -yonē? -よねえ？, i.e. asking the other person to confirm your opinion. Only people under the age of about 35 use -jan.

What you did was stupid! Baka-da!

ばかだ！

You're crazy!   Ikareten-janai-no?

いかれてんじゃないの？

Kichigai!

気違い！

Stop acting stupid/   Fuzakenai-deyo! ♀
   Don't joke around   ふざけないでよ！
   with me!   Fuzakeruna-yo! ♂

ふざけるなよ！

Used in cases where someone is acting stupidly or has said something stupid.

Fuzaken-ja nēyo! ♂
ふざけんじゃねえよ！

This is especially used when someone is being cheeky or has underestimated the speaker's power or status.

Don't act stupid/
  Stop acting stupid!

Baka yamete-yo! ♀
ばか止めてよ！
Baka yamero-yo! ♂
ばか止めろよ！
Baka yamena-yo! ♀
ばか止めなよ！
Baka yatten-ja nēyo! ♂
ばかやってんじゃねえよ！

These phrases can all be used when someone pisses you off. Phrases beginning with *baka* ("stupid," "crazy") can also be voiced with concern for a friend's silly, irrational behavior.

Don't say (such) stupid
  things!

Baka iwanai-deyo! ♀
ばか言わないでよ！
Baka ittenna-yo! ♂
ばか言ってんなよ！
Netenna-yo! ♂
寝てんなよ！

Netenna-yo! literally means "Wake up!"

Liar!

Usotsuki!
嘘つき！

You've got a big mouth!

Oshaberi!
おしゃべり！

Someone who's always spreading the latest rumor, people's secrets, etc.

Get your head out of
  your ass!

Neboken-ja nēyo! ♂
寝ぼけんじゃねえよ！

Literally means "Aren't you half-asleep (because of what you did/are doing)?" Depending upon your tone of voice, this phrase can be very funny or very harsh.

That's a lie!

Sonna-no uso-da!
そんなの嘘だ！
Sonna-no uso-dayo!
そんなの嘘だよ！
Uso bakkari!
嘘ばっかり！

Don't lie!

Uso tsukanai-deyo! ♀
嘘つかないでよ！
Uso tsukuna-yo! ♂
嘘つくなよ！

Stop it!

Yamete-yo! ♀
止めてよ！
Yamero-yo! ♂
止めろよ！

You shouldn't do that/ Don't do that!

Dame!
だめ！
Dame-dayo! ♂
だめだよ！

Why do you do things like that?

Nande sonna-koto suru-no?
何でそんな事するの？

Why did you do such a thing?

Nande sonna-koto shita-no?
何でそんな事したの？

Leave him/her alone!

Hottoite-agete! ♀
ほっといてあげて！
Hottoite-yare-yo! ♂
ほっといてやれよ！
Hottoke-yo! ♂
ほっとけよ！

Do as I say!

Itta-tōri-ni shite! ♀
言った通りにして！
Itta-tōri-ni shiro-yo! ♂
言った通りにしろよ！

This is the limit!

Ii kagen-ni shite-yo!
いいかげんにしてよ！
Ii kagen-ni shiro-yo! ♂
いいかげんにしろよ！

Stop it!

Shitsukoi!
しつこい！

When someone is being persistent.

Give it back!

Kaeshite-yo!
返してよ！
Kaeshite-kure! ♂
返してくれ！
Kaese-yo! ♂
返せよ！

Leave me alone!

Hottoite-yo! ♀
ほっといてよ！
Hottoite-kure-yo! ♂
ほっといてくれよ！

Leave us alone!

Atashitachi-dake-ni shite-yo! ♀
あたしたちだけにしてよ！
Bokutachi-dake-ni
shite-kure-yo! ♂
僕達だけにしてくれよ！

Get out of here/
Fuck off!

Kiero! ♂
きえろ！
Mukō itte-yo! ♀
向こうに行ってよ！
Acchi itte-yo! ♀
あっち行ってよ！
Acchi ike-yo! ♂
あっち行けよ！
Dokka icchimae! ♂
どっか行っちまえ！
Dokka itte-yo! ♀
どっか行ってよ！
Dokka ike-yo! ♂
どっか行けよ！
Hayaku inakunare-yo! ♂
早くいなくなれよ！
Urochoro shitenna! ♂
うろちょろしてんな！
Totto-to usero! ♂
とっととうせろ！

Come here!

Chotto kocchi kite! ♀
ちょっとこっち来て！
Kocchi oide-yo! ♀ (b→g)
こっちおいでよ！
Kocchi koi-yo! ♂
こっち来いよ！

You're noisy!

Urusai!
うるさい！
Urusē-na! ♂
うるせえな！
Urusē-yo! m
うるせえよ！
Urusēn-dayo! ♂
うるせえんだよ！

Shut up! Damatte-yo! ♀
黙ってよ！
Damare-yo! ♂
黙れよ！

Stop your babbling! Gocha-gocha/
Gata-gata itten-ja nēyo! ♂
ごちゃごちゃ／
がたがた言ってんじゃねえよ！

Be quiet! Shizuka-ni shite-yo! ♀ (b→g)
静かにしてよ！
Shizuka-ni shiro-yo! ♂
静かにしろよ！

Both phrases can be used playfully between boyfriend and girlfriend. In a movie theater, pub, etc., you should first say *Shizuka-ni shite kudasai* 静かにしてくだ下さい. If there are no results, *Shizuka-ni shite-yo!* or *Shizuka-ni shiro-yo!* should do the trick. Still no progress? Throw in a couple of *Urusen-dayo!*'s.

You asshole! Kono kuso-ttare! ♂
このくそったれ！

Literally means "You have shit around your asshole!"

You bitch! Kono kuso-onna! ♂ (b/g→g)
このくそ女！

You whore!   Yariman! (b/g→g)
                                  やりまん！

This means a girl who will go to bed with anyone.

Home boy!   Dasai!
                                  ダサい！
                                  Kono imo!
                                  このイモ！

Kono imo! literally means "You potato!" and comes from the fact that potatoes are grown in the country. You can also say *ikete-nai* いけてない You're saying they are unfashionable, or that their talk is uncool.

Playboy!   Pureibōi! (g→b)
                                  プレイボーイ！

A bad word to say to boys.

Shorty!   Chibi!
                                  ちび！
                                  Gaki!
                                  がき！

Short legs!   Tansoku!
                                  短足！

Weakling!   Yowa-mushi!
                                  弱むし！

You ain't got balls!   Konjō nashi!
                                  根性なし！

Means you're lacking in the "brave" department.

                                  Chinchin chiisai! ♂
                                  ちんちん小さい！

This literally means "You have a small penis!" As you'd expect, this is a very serious insult!

You're ugly!　　　　　　Busu! (ugly girl) (b/g→g)
　　　　　　　　　　　　ぶす！
　　　　　　　　　　　　Busaiku! (both)
　　　　　　　　　　　　不細工！

Busaiku! is the worst word to say to a girl.

You pig!　　　　　　　Buta!
　　　　　　　　　　　　豚！
　　　　　　　　　　　　Debu!
　　　　　　　　　　　　でぶ！

Said to girls and to obese boys.

Fag!　　　　　　　　　Okama!
　　　　　　　　　　　　おかま！

Said to a boy who acts or dresses in a feminine manner.

Tomboy!　　　　　　　Otoko onna!
　　　　　　　　　　　　男女！
　　　　　　　　　　　　Otemba!
　　　　　　　　　　　　おてんば！

This is an uncommon insult in Japan.

White boy!　　　　　　Haku-jin!
　　　　　　　　　　　　白人！

You're the lowest!　　　Saitei!
　　　　　　　　　　　　最低！
　　　　　　　　　　　　Saitei-dayo!
　　　　　　　　　　　　最低だよ！

You're narrow-minded!　Kokoro(-ga) semai yo nē!
　　　　　　　　　　　　心(が)狭いよねえ。

Don't be so cocky!　　　Erasō-ni suruna-yo!
　　　　　　　　　　　　偉そうにするなよ！

You're a tightwad!   Kechi!
                                けち！
                                Do-kechi!
                                どけち！

Do-kechi is even tighter than *kechi*, which is already a strong word.

You're a dirtbag!   Kitanai!
                                汚い！

Don't fuck with me!   Namen-ja nēyo! ♂
                                なめんじゃねえよ！

This literally means "Don't lick me!" If someone says *Nandayo?* 何だよ？to you, you could just say one of the above and walk away (as the winner). But the Japanese themselves don't use this that much. Less direct insults can have more effect.

If you don't have time to "socialize," just fire off one or two of these parting shots. *Baka!* ばか！(You're stupid!); *Baka-mitai!* ばかみたい！(You look stupid!); *Yanayatsu!* ♀ やなやつ！(What a nasty person!); *Henna-yatsu!* ♂ 変なやつ！(What a geek!); *Henna-yarō!* ♂ 変なやろう！(What a chump!); *Baka-ja nēno!* ♂ ばかじゃねえの！(How stupid!); *Baka-jan!* ♂ ばかじゃん！(That's so stupid!).

Fuck you!/Go to hell!
Kutabare! ♂
くたばれ！
Shine! ♂
死ね！

Don't try to be cool!
Kakko tsukenna-yo! ♂
かっこ付けんなよ！

Let's finish this now!
Keri- o tsuke-yōze! ♂
けりをつけようぜ！

I'm going to kick your ass!
Bukkoroshite yaru! ♂
ぶっ殺してやる！
Korosuzo! ♂
殺すぞ！

These literally mean "I'm going to hit you till you die!" and "I'm going to kill you!" They're harsh phrases—expect to throw a few punches after you say them!

You dog!
Kono-yarō! ♂
このやろう！

Serious fighting words! Usually said before or while the right hook is connecting.

That hurts!
Itai!
痛い！
Itē-na! ♂
痛えな！

These phrases are said to ensure the offender knows you're hurt. *Itai* is said when you've been made to hurt yourself.

You little rat!
(Check this geek out!)
Nani koitsu!
何こいつ？

Said about anyone doing anything, but usually not to their face.

Who do you think you are?!

Nani-sama no tsumori?! ♀
何様のつもり？！
Anta nani-sama na-no?!
あんた何様なの？！
Nani temē?! ♂
何てめえ？！

Anta is a shorter way for girls to say *anata* "you," and in the Kanto area, *anta* is considered to be harsher than *anata*. The first two phrases are mockingly disrespectful, and *temē* is a bad boy's word for "you." *Nani temē*?! can be said to their face—with care!

Street Fighting

Street Fighting

9

Have you ever noticed that while you're waiting in line for something—it doesn't matter what—for some reason people seem to think their position is at the front of the line? The following phrases should get your point across.

We're making a line.	Naranderun-dakedo. 並んでるんだけど。
Don't push!	Osanai-deyo! ♀ 押さないでよ！ Osuna-yo! ♂ 押すなよ！
What's this old man doing?!	Nani kono jijii?! 何このじじい?! Nanda-yo kono jijii?! 何だよこのじじい?!

Jiji is from (the much politer form) *ojii-san* (grandfather/old man).

What's this old woman doing?!	Nani kono babā?! 何このばばあ?! Nanda-yo kono babā?! 何だよこのばばあ?!

Babā is from (the again much politer form) *obā-san* (grandmother/old woman).

Man, they're slow!	Osoi-nē. 遅いねえ。 Osoi-nā. ♂ 遅いなあ。
Could you go a bit faster?	Mō chotto hayaku...? もうちょっと速く。

The service here is bad.   Koko no sābisu wa yokunai.
ここのサービスはよくない。

Do you want to say   Nanka-iitai-no?!
something?!   何か言いたいの？！

The Japanese are infamous for staring, especially at things foreign
or unusual. To have them return to their own affairs, a simple
Nanda-yo?! 何だよ？！ or *Nanka yō*?! 何かよう？！works well.
But then again, the Japanese are also known for their persistence.
If these two fail, simply tell them:

Don't look at me!   (Kocchi) minaide-yo! ♀
（こっち）見ないでよ！
(Kocchi) miruna-yo! ♂
（こっち）見るなよ！
Miten-ja nēyo! ♂
見てんじゃねえよ！

Don't stare at me!   Jiro jiro minai-deyo! ♀
ジロジロ見ないでよ！
Jiro jiro miruna-yo! ♂
ジロジロ見るなよ！

These phrases can be used in most situations to get your point
across forcefully.

Gan tobashiten-ja nēyo! ♂
がんとばしてんじゃねえよ！

This last phrase is very strong, usually only used when you really
hate someone or you're about to start a fight with them!

Chikan(!)   Chikan(!)
                                 ちかん（！）

Women in Japan need to watch out for *chikan*, who are strangers who enjoys doing perverse sexual acts. They like to touch any part of the woman's body, put their body against the woman's, to "flash"—and foreign women are targets as well. The *chikan* act fearlessly in public, usually riding the train during the morning and late afternoon rush hours to benefit from the closeness of the passengers. Most girls will freak out, and the few who don't might slap the offender and/or accuse him of sexual harassment. The *chikan* might counter-attack with *Dare-ga omae-nanka sawaru-kayo?!* ♂ 誰がお前なんか触るかよ？！ Who would want to touch you?!

The sad part is that no one will come to the rescue—the people on the train will quietly look away as if nothing happened. For a guy who would like to score a few "brownie points," give your assistance in a situation like this. Everyone will be surprised— probably even more surprised than the *chikan*. But if Superman isn't around the corner, your only fallback is to use the following words/phrases and the others listed in this chapter.

Lewd! Vulgar!   Sukebe! ♀
                                すけべ！

Sexual perversion/   Hentai.
  Abnormality.   変態。

Placing *kono* この in front of *sukebe* and *hentai* will direct the attention to one person, such as *Kono sukebe!* (You freak!) and *Kono hentai!* (You pervert!)

Take your hand(s) off!   Te dokete-yo! ♀
                                手どけてよ！

Don't touch me!   Sawannai-de! ♀
                                触んないで！

You're dirty!   Kitanai-wane! ♀
                                汚いわね！

A couple of years ago, we went to a club in Tokyo. As I was about to pay the cover charge, I was told our fee was almost twice the norm! There was no doubt in my mind as to why, but I became so irate we just left. However, the second time this happened we settled the problem right away.

If this happens to you (and it may not—some clubs see foreigners as desirable, drawing in other Japanese customers), and you are determined to patronize the place, the first thing you should do is let them know you speak and understand Japanese. That should throw them off-guard, reducing the chance of them continuing the scheme. Say anything relating to the situation, because they know what you're talking about. If they ask you questions, don't worry about answering them. Just keep stressing what you want. If they don't give in, do what you would do back home—call for the manager!

But just make sure that you are actually being ripped off before you let fly with phrases like these! Some Japanese clubs can be very pricey, by Western and even by Japanese standards. This is where having "local knowledge" is vital—either gained or by having Japanese friends with you.

This can't be right!	Kore wa hontō janai deshō! ♀
	これは本当じゃないでしょう！
	Kore wa hontō janai darō! ♂
	これは本当じゃないだろう！

This is slightly politer than the blunt phrases in YES AND NO. Choose your level of impact!

I think you are trying to trick me!	Damasō-to shiteru deshō! ♀
	だまそうとしてるでしょう！
	Damasō-to shiterun-darō! ♂
	だまそうとしてるんだろう！

This can't be so expensive!	Konna-ni takai-wake nai!
	こんなに高い訳ない！
	Botterun-darō! ♂
	ぼってるんだろう！

This is different from what I've heard!	Kiita hanashi-to chigaun dakedo! 聞いた話と違うんだけど！ Kiita hanashi-to chigau-yo! 聞いた話と違うよ！
If you think I don't know anything, you're wrong!	Damasarenai-wayo! ♀ だまされないわよ！ Damasarenai-yo! ♂ だまされないよ！
Don't think I'm stupid!	Baka-ni shinai-deyo! ♀ ばかにしないでよ！ Baka-ni suruna-yo! ♂ ばかにするなよ！
Explain to me why!	Setsumei shite! 説明して！ Setsumei shite-kureru?! 説明してくれる？！
Think about it!	Kangaete-mite! ♀ 考えてみて！ Kangaete-mina! ♂ 考えてみな！
Don't you think you're wrong?	Jibun-de warui-to omowanai-no? 自分で悪いと思わないの？
Is this because I'm a foreigner?	Gaikoku-jin dakara? 外国人だから？
Is this because I'm an American?	Amerika-jin dakara? アメリカ人だから？
I want to talk to the manager!	Manējā yon-deyo! ♀ マネージャー呼んでよ！ Manējā yonde-kure-yo! ♂ マネージャー呼んでくれよ！

I won't come here again!

Mō nido-to konai!
もう二度と来ない！
Mō nido-to konai-yo! ♂
もう二度と来ないよ！

I'll tell all my friends!

Minna ni iu kara!
皆に言うから！
Minna ni iu yo! ♂
皆に言うよ！

Hey! Tell me your name!

Chotto! Namae oshiete-yo! ♀
ちょっと！名前教えてよ！
Chotto! Namae oshiero-yo! ♂
ちょっと！名前教えろよ！

You better remember
what you tried to do!

Oboete-nasai-yo! ♀
覚えてなさいよ！

You won't get away
with this!

Oboetero-yo! ♂
覚えてろよ！

Check It Out!

Look!	Mite! 見て！
Look at this!	Kore mite! これ見て！
Look at that!	Are mite! あれ見て！
Take a look.	Chotto mite. ちょっと見て。
Don't look!	Minaide! 見ないで！ Miruna-yo! ♂ 見るなよ！
I'll show you.	Misete ageru. 見せてあげる。 Miseru. 見せる。
I won't show you.	Misete agenai. 見せてあげない。 Misenai. 見せない。
Did you see (it)?	Mita? 見た？

I saw (it).　　　　　　　Mita-mita.
　　　　　　　　　　　　　見た見た

This is a (usually feminine) emphatic form, which normally shows enthusiasm.

　　　　　　　　　　　　　Mita.
　　　　　　　　　　　　　見た。
　　　　　　　　　　　　　Mita-yo.
　　　　　　　　　　　　　見たよ。

I didn't see (it).　　　　Minakatta.
　　　　　　　　　　　　　見なかった。

I couldn't see (it).　　　Mienakatta.
　　　　　　　　　　　　　見えなかった。

When you can't see something because something else is in the way.

　　　　　　　　　　　　　Mirenakatta.
　　　　　　　　　　　　　見れなかった。

When you can't see something because of your own lack of vision or perception.

I don't want to see (it).　Mitakunai.
　　　　　　　　　　　　　見たくない。

Do you want to see...?　...Mitai?
　　　　　　　　　　　　　...見たい？

Shall we go and see it?　Mite miyō-ka?
　　　　　　　　　　　　　見てみようか？

This is of course a good phrase when thinking about movies. The movies in Japan are quite expensive, and with most theaters downtown, are not such a popular option for people in the suburbs. With the proliferation of home theater systems, many people now borrow videos or DVDs instead.

**Shall we get a video/
DVD (instead)?**

(Sono kawari) Bideo/DVD o
    karite miyō-ka?
（その代わり）ビデオ・DVDを借
    りてみようか。

There are plenty of other socializing options though, with perhaps
the most common being shopping, karaoke and going drinking or
clubbing.

Shall we go shopping?

Shoppingu shi-ni ikō-ka.
ショッピングしに行こうか。

**Let's go (shopping in)
Ginza/Umeda.**

Ginza/Umeda-de shoppingu shiyō.
銀座／梅田でショッピング
しよう。

**I want to go shopping
for clothes.**

Yōfuku-o kaitai.
洋服を買いたい。

In Japan, you usually go social shopping downtown, in the big (and
attractive, especially to women!) department stores (such as
Ginza in Tokyo and Umeda in Osaka) and specialty shopping
districts (e.g. Tokyo's Akihabara is famed for its electronics shops).
Suburban malls, which are not nearly as big as in the US, are for
more mundane clothes or food shopping.

A casual evening or night out in Japan will often involve karaoke.

Do you like karaoke?

Karaoke suki?
カラオケ好き？

Let's sing karaoke.　　　　Karaoke utaō/ikō.
　　　　　　　　　　　　　　　カラオケ歌おう／行こう。

Karaoke literally means "without orchestra." You usually sing in special karaoke "bars" dotted around cities but especially in major railway stations and entertainment areas. The "bars" are collections of many rooms, where you can sing, eat and drink in relative privacy. The singing itself consists of individuals/pairs/groups singing the vocals of their favorite songs, backed by digitised instruments. Like all their fun, Japanese take this very seriously.

You can get drinks in karaoke bars, but many places are dedicated to alcohol.

Shall we go bowling?　　　　Bōringu ni ikō-ka?
　　　　　　　　　　　　　　　ボーリングに行こうか。

Shall we go to the game　　Gēmu sentā ni ikō-ka?
center?　　　　　　　　　　ゲームセンターに行こうか。

Game centers are common in Japan and are where kids can go and play video-games, air-hockey, do "print clubs" *purikura* プリクラ (taking photos of yourself and making funny stickers out of them). They are big, noisy and fun places. But older kids might prefer the following options.

Shall we go (for a drink) drinking?	(Chotto) Nomi-ni ikō-ka? （ちょっと）飲みに行こうか。
I wonder where we should go.	Doko ga ii kanā. どこがいいかなあ。
Do you know a good place (near here)?	(Kono hen-ni) ii tokoro aru? （この辺に）いい所ある？
I know a good place.	Aru(-yo). ある（よ）。

Drinking is a vital social activity in Japan, where the inhibitions of the day can be partially cast aside in a friendlier environment than the workplace. "After-work" drinks are usually at a local *izakaya* 居酒屋, or, in summer, an outdoor beer hall. Small *izakaya* are numerous, and they provide good food as well as plenty of beer, whisky (or whatever!) They are often quite "Japanese-y" inside, with low tables to sit at, encouraging close conversation and a lively atmosphere. There are more and more Western-style bars these days, but they're mainly in downtown entertainment areas.

Serious nights out involve going downtown, to nightclub districts like *Roppongi* and *Kabukichō* in Tokyo and *Minami* and *Shinsaibashi* in Osaka, where there are incredible arrays of bars, clubs and parlors catering to (literally) every taste. But because the trains and buses don't run from about midnight to 6 a.m., if you don't live nearby or have lots of money for a taxi, it pays to plan ahead!

Shall we go clubbing this Friday/Saturday?	Kinyōbi/Doyōbi-ni kurabu toka ni ikō-ka? 金曜日／土曜日にクラブとかに行こうか。
What sort of club should we go to?	Donna kurabu ga ii? どんなクラブがいい？

Let's go to your favorite club.

Anata-no yoku iku kurabu-ni ikō.♀
あなたのよく行くクラブに行こう。
Kimi-no yoku iku kurabu-ni
ikō-yō. ♂
君のよく行くクラブに行こうよ。

Use *yoku iku* to indicate a place you often go to.

Chitchat 11

Are you having a good time?

Tanoshinderu?
楽しんでる？

If someone says *Tanoshinderu?* to you, the best answer is *Un* or *Mane,* meaning "Yeah, I am."

You look like you're having a good time.

◆ Tanoshisō-dane.
楽しそうだね。

Yeah, I'm having fun.

Tanoshii-yo.
楽しいよ。

No, not really.

Mā, sō-ne.
まあ、そうね。
Anmari.
あんまり。
Betsu-ni.
別に。

Mā, sō-ne can indicate either (indifferent) agreement or subtle disagreement (subtle being the best disagreement in this situation!) depending on how you say it. Saying it with a lack of enthusiasm, or the latter two, will show that you're not really enjoying yourself. And of course this hints that you'd rather move on or go home!

We're having a good time, aren't we?	Tanoshii-nē? 楽しいねえ？

Did you two come here by yourselves?	Futari-de kiteru-no? 二人で来てるの？

If more than two people, replace *futari* with *san-nin* 三人 (three), *yo-nin* 四人 (four) etc.

Shall we drink together?	Issho-ni nomanai? 一緒に飲まない？

"Shall we drink together?" doesn't quite make the top 100 list of all-time great pick-up lines, but nonetheless, it's very effective in Japan. If the mood is right and someone is eyeballing you, this is a good one to get the party going (or at least to sit at their table).

Has someone reserved this seat?	Kono seki aiteru? この席空いてる？

This is a clever way to say "May I sit here?"

Is someone sitting here?	Koko dare-ka suwatteru? ここ誰か座ってる？

Do you want to sit down?	Suwaranai? 座らない？

May I sit down?	Suwatte-mo-ii? 座ってもいい？

Let me sit down.	Suwarasete. 座らせて。

Shuffle over/Make room.	Tsumete. つめて。 Chotto ii? ちょっといい？

Chotto ii? literally means "Excuse me, okay?" You should point or look at the seat to make yourself clear.

What's your name?   Namae nante iu-no?
名前何て言うの？

Guess what it is!   Atete mite!
あててみて！
Nanda-to omou?
何だと思う？

You might hear these two if you ask a personal question. Either they're playing with you or they really don't want you to know. You have to read their body language!

What did you say?   Nante itta-no?
何て言ったの？
Nani?
何？
E?
え？
Nante ittan-dayo? ♂
何て言ったんだよ？

Nante ittan-dayo? is quite accusative, and is not to be used in a delicate situation, or when you're trying to make friends!

Where do you live?   Doko-ni sunderu-no?
どこに住んでるの？

Where do you come from? Dokkara kita-no?
どっから来たの？

Doko-ni sunderu-no? should be used if you are introduced by someone. If there is no introduction, both *Doko-ni sunderu-no?* and *Dokkara kita-no?* are okay and both produce the same answer. Girls might tell you their address, or they may just say *atchi* あっち, meaning "Over there."

How old are you? Nansai?
何歳？

To this question, girls will usually answer with *Atete! Nansai-da-to omou?* あてて！何歳だと思う？Guess! How old do you think I am?, or *Ikutsu-ni mieru?* いくつに見える？How old do I look?

Are you a student? Gakusei?
学生？

The answer might be *daigakusei* 大学生 (university student), *sen-mon-gakkōsei* 専門学校生 (student of a specialist school e.g. dental assistant, nurse etc).

Where are you studying (i.e. at what institution)? Doko-de benkyō shiteru-no?
どこで勉強してるの？

What's your job? Shigoto nani shiten-no?
仕事何してんの？

How do you spend your time? Itsumo nani shiten-no?
いつも何してんの？

Do you come here often? Yoku koko kuru-no?
よくここ来るの？

Have I seen you before? Mae-ni atta-koto attakke?
前に会ったことあったっけ？

Your English is good.   Eigo umai-ne.
英語うまいね。

While introducing yourself to a Japanese, you could try getting them to speak a bit in English, and ingratiate yourself with this and the other phrases in SAY WHAT? Even if the conversation continues in Japanese, you'll have kicked off on the right foot!

What music do you like?   Donna ongaku-ga suki?
どんな音楽が好き？

Whose music do you like?   Dare-no ongaku-ga suki?
誰の音楽が好き？

Do you know this song?   Kono uta/kyoku shitteru?
この歌／曲知ってる？

I know it.   Shitteru.
知ってる。
Shitteru-yo.
知ってるよ。

I don't know it.   Shiranai.
知らない。
Shiran. ♂
知らん。

Shall we dance?   Odoranai?
踊らない？

I don't feel like dancing yet.   Mada odoru-ki shinai.
まだ踊る気しない。
Mada odoranai.
まだ踊らない。

You're a good dancer.   Dansu umai-ne.
ダンスうまいね。

How do you know of this place?	Nande koko shitten-no? 何でここ知ってんの？
I heard from my friends.	Tomodachi-ni kiita. 友達に聞いた。 Tomodachi-ni kiitan-da. ♂ 友達に聞いたんだ。
Where else do you go to dance?	Hoka-ni donna kurabu-ni iku-no? 他にどんなクラブに行くの？
How long have you been in Japan?	Dono-gurai Nihon-ni iru-no? どのぐらい日本にいるの？
Do you like Japanese girls/boys?	Nihon-no onnanoko/otokonoko suki? 日本の女の子／男の子好き？

Let's party!	Tanoshimō-yo! 楽しもうよ！
Let's get drunk!	Konya-wa nomō! 今夜は飲もう！ Yopparaō! 酔っ払おう！ Moriagarō! もりあがろう！

What are you drinking?   Nani nonden-no?
何飲んでるの？

Have you been drinking   Kanari nonderu?
a lot?   かなり飲んでる？

Well, drink some more.   Jā, motto nomeba!
じゃあ、もっと飲めば！

You need to drink more.   Motto nomina-yo!
もっと飲みなよ！

You can handle your   ◆ Osake tsuyoi-ne.
drink, can't you?   お酒強いね。

Are you drunk?   Yotteru?
酔ってる？

Haven't you drunk   Nomisugi-janai?
too much?   飲み過ぎじゃない？

Maybe you should   Mō nomu-no yametara.
stop drinking.   もう飲むの止めたら。

Are you okay?   Daijōbu?
大丈夫？

You're kind.   ◆ Yasashii-ne.
優しいね。

What time did you   Nanji-goro kita-no?
come here?   何時ごろ来たの？

What time is your   Mongen nanji?
curfew?   門限何時？

What time are you leaving?	Nanji-goro kaeru-no? 何時ごろ帰るの？
I haven't decided.	Kimetenai. 決めてない。
If I have a good time, I'll stay.	Tanoshikattara iru. 楽しかったらいる。
If this gets boring, I'll go (home).	Tsumannakattara kaeru. つまんなかったら帰る。
I'll help you to have a good time.	Issho-ni tanoshimō-yo. 一緒に楽しもうよ。
This is boring!	Omoshirokunai! 面白くない！ Tsumannai! つまんない！ Tsumannē! ♂ つまんねえ！

The latter two, if said slowly, are clever ways to say "What you said isn't funny!" or "Your joke is stupid!" They are also adjectives with certain nouns: *Tsumannai yatsu!* つまんないやつ！You're boring! or He/she's boring!; *Tsumannē eiga* ♂ つまんねえ映画. This is a boring movie etc.

Shall we go somewhere else?	Dokka ikanai? どっか行かない？
Shall we leave?	Denai? 出ない？
Can my friends come?	Tomodachi-mo issho-de ii? 友達も一緒でいい？
I'd like to stay here longer.	Mada koko-ni itai. まだここにいたい。
What's next?	Kono ato dō-suru-no? この後どうするの？
Have you decided?	Kimatta? 決まった？
I haven't decided yet.	Mada kimetenai. まだ決めてない。
It's up to you.	Makaseru. 任せる。 Makaseru-yo. 任せるよ。
Anything's fine.	Nan-demo ii. 何でもいい。 Nan-demo ii-yo. なんでもいいよ。
Either will do.	Docchi-demo ii. どっちでもいい。 Docchi-demo ii-yo. どっちでもいいよ。

I have a good idea.

Ii kangae ga aru.
いい考えがある。
Ii koto kangaeta.
いい事考えた。

How does that sound?

Sore-de ii?
それでいい？
Dō?
どう？

Good idea.

Guddo aidia!
グッド・アイディア！

You've got your head on straight today, haven't you?

Kyō saeteru-nē?
今日さえてるねえ。

I've got my head on straight today.

Kyō saeteru.
今日さえてる。

Anywhere's okay.

Doko-demo ii.
どこでもいい。
Doko-demo ii-yo.
どこでもいいよ。

I'll take you home.	Okutte ku-yo. 送ってくよ。 Okutte iku-yo. 送って行くよ。
I wanna know more about you.	Anata-no-koto motto shiritai. ♀ あなたの事もっと知りたい。 Kimi-no-koto motto shiritai. ♂ 君の事もっと知りたい。
Do you want to drink morning coffee together?	Issho-ni yoake-no kōhii nomanai? 一緒によあけのコーヒー飲まない？

An old way to ask if you want to spend the night together (in bed, of course).

We think the same way, don't we?	Ki-ga au-nē? 気が合うねえ？
Shall we meet again?	Mata aeru? また会える？
When can I see you next time?	Kondo itsu aeru? 今度いつ会える？
May I call you?	Denwa shite-mo ii? 電話してもいい？
May I have your phone number?	Denwa bangō oshiete-kureru? 電話番号教えてくれる？
Do you have something to write with?	Nanka kaku-mono aru? 何か書く物ある？

I enjoyed myself.　　Tanoshikatta.
楽しかった。

Take care.　　Ki-o-tsukete-ne.
気を付けてね。

See you later.　　Jā mata-ne.
じゃあまたね。
Mata-ne.
またね。
Jā ne.
じゃあね。

See you tomorrow.　　Jā mata ashita-ne.
じゃあまた明日ね。
Mata ashita-ne.
また明日ね。
Jā ashita-ne.
じゃあ明日ね。

Bye (bye)!　　Bai bāi!
バイバーイ！

On the Phone

12

Phone communication is very important to the Japanese. With transport being relatively slow in such a densely-populated country, keeping in touch electronically is the most effective way to maintain relationships. And as email has taken off a lot slower than in the West, with older generations especially, the phone is still a lifeline.

Hello(?)

Moshi-moshi(?)
もしもし？

As with other often-used phrases, everyone has their own way to say *moshi-moshi*, from the musical to the interrogative. Find your style!

Is...there please?

...san wa imaska?
…さんはいますか。
...(wa) iru?
…(は)いる？

Could you get...please?

...san-ni kawatte-kuremaska?
…さんに変わってくれますか？
...ni kawatte-kureru?
…に変わってくれる？

Hold on please.

Shō-shō omachi kudasai.
少々お待ち下さい。

This is a very formal phrase, but one you might hear when a stranger answers the phone.

Chotto matte kudasai.
ちょっと待って下さい。
Chotto mattete.
ちょっと待ってて。

Calling someone's house when you don't know who might answer is one of those times you really should use the *mas* form. Calling a mobile phone of course solves this problem!

The Japanese have been the world's most enthusiastic adopters of mobile phones, with all young and more and more older people being connected. Aggressive marketing and product development mean that they have a huge choice of feature-packed *keitai denwa* 携帯電話 (usually just *keitai* 携帯), which (though of similar colors) are all light and compact with screen sizes increasing all the time. This helps with the most important feature of the phones, the text messaging, or *mēru*.

Young Japanese in particular spend hours (especially otherwise wasted time on the train) each day emailing their friends via their phones, and having one is now a necessity, not a luxury. With full and fast *kanji* input and low costs (usually 1 yen per message), the *mēru* culture has taken hold. And your phone is very much a form of personal expression. What trinkets you attach to it and what music plays when a call or message arrives defines who you are and what fashions you follow.

What kind of phone did you buy?

Donna keitai katta-no?
どんな携帯買ったの？

This (attachment) is really cute.

Kore, sugoku kawaii.
これ、すごくかわいい。

What's your email address?

Adoresu wa?
アドレスは？

This is a cue for some good *katakana*-ized pronunciation practice—or frantic scribbling!

Can you do email in English/Japanese?

Eigo/Nihongo-de mēru dekiru?
英語／日本語でメールできる？

Please email me in English/Japanese.

Eigo/Nihongo-de mēru kureru?
英語／日本語でメールくれる？

It's hard to email with this phone.

Kono keitai-no mēru wakarinikui.
この携帯のメール分かりにくい。

Could you teach me?

(Chotto) Oshiete-kureru?
（ちょっと）教えてくれる？

But even if you *mēru* like crazy, every now and then you will still have to call someone. Here are some useful phrases.

How are you doing?

Genki?
元気？

I've been doing okay.

Genki-dayo.
元気だよ。

If you want to put these two phrases together, asking how the other person is and saying you're okay in the same breath, for clarity you should say *Genki? Atashi-wa/Boku-wa genki-dayo*, adding the subject (me) to the second phrase.

So-so/Not good, not bad.   Mā-mā.
まあまあ。

What were you doing?   Nani shiteta-no?
何してたの？

You're late.   ◆ Osoi-ne.
遅いね。

I tried to call you.   Denwashita-noyo.
電話したのよ。

My (phone's) battery was flat.   Batterii-ga kireta.
バッテリーが切れた。

The line was busy.   Hanashichū datta.
話中だった。

Who was on the phone?   Dare-ga denwa tsukatteta-no?
誰が電話使ってたの？

I want to see you.   Aitai.
会いたい。

I want to see you now.   Ima-sugu aitai.
今すぐ会いたい。

I'll call you again.

Mata kakeru-ne.
またかけるね。
Mata denwa suru-ne.
また電話するね。

I'll call you after I get there (to the station).

(Eki ni) tsuite kara denwa suru-ne.
(駅に)着いてから電話するね。

What time can I call tomorrow?

Ashita nanji-ni denwa shite ii?
明日何時に電話していい。

I'll call tomorrow at 6 o'clock.

Ashita rokuji-ni denwa suru-ne.
明日6時に電話するね。

Please be home.

Ie-ni ite kudasai.
家にいて下さい。

Will you be on (internet) chat tomorrow?

Ashita (intānetto) chatto-ni deru?
明日(インターネット)チャットに
出る。

Say hello to Hisako for me.

Hisako-ni yoroshiku-ne.
ひさこによろしくね。

Lovers' Language 13

I'm crazy about you.

Sugoku suki.
すごく好き。

I love you.

Aishiteru.
愛してる。

I'm yours.

Atashi-wa anata-no kanojo/mono. ♀
あたしはあなたの彼女／もの。
Boku-wa kimi-no kareshi. ♂
僕は君の彼氏。

You're mine.

Anata-wa atashi-no kareshi. ♀
あなたはあたしの彼氏。
Kimi-wa boku-no kanojo. ♂
君は僕の彼女。

I want to know all about you.

Anata-no-koto zembu shiritai. ♀
あなたの事全部知りたい。
Kimi-no-koto zembu shiritai. ♂
君の事全部知りたい。

I'll tell you.

Oshiete-ageru.
教えてあげる。

You look beautiful.

Kirei-dayo. (b→g)
きれいだよ。

You're attractive.

Suteki-yo.
すてきよ。
Suteki-dayo. (b→g)
すてきだよ。

You're sexy!

Sekushii-dane.
セクシーだね。

Look at me.

Kocchi mite.
こっち見て。

You have beautiful eyes.

Kirei-na me-dane. ♂
きれいな目だね。

You're quiet aren't you?

Otonashii-ne?
おとなしいね？

You smell sweet.

Ii kaori.
いい香り。

May I kiss you?

Kisu shite-mo ii?
キスしてもいい？

Kiss me.

Kisu shite.
キスして。

Where?

Doko-ni?
どこに？

May I love you? Aishite-mo ii?
愛してもいい？

This has two meanings, "May I make love to you?" and "May I give you my heart?"

Don't be shy. Hazukashi-garanai-de.
恥ずかしがらないで。

Close your eyes. Me-o tojite.
目を閉じて。

I'm embarrassed. Hazukashii.
恥ずかしい。

You have a beautiful body. Kirei-na karada-dane. ♂
きれいな体だね。

Will you look the other way for a second? Chotto acchi muitete?
ちょっとあっち向いてて。

Is this your first time? Hajimete?
初めて？

Tell me the truth. Hontō-no-koto itte.
本当の事言って。

Don't worry. Shimpai shinai-de.
心配しないで。

It's gonna be okay. Daijōbu(-dayo).
大丈夫(だよ)。

Treat me kindly. Yasashiku shite-ne. ♀
優しくしてね。

Is today safe for you? Kyō wa daijōbu-na hi? ♂
今日は大丈夫な日？

**I don't want to have
a baby.**

Aka-chan hoshikunai-no. ♀
赤ちゃん欲しくないの。

Will you use a condom?

Gomu tsukete? ♀
ゴムつけて？

I'll use a condom.

Gomu tsukeru. ♂
ゴムつける。

Are you on the Pill?

Piru nonderu? ♂
ビル飲んでる？

The Pill became available in Japan well after the West, and is not very widely used. Its use is sometimes associated with depression, so guys may be better off assuming that she isn't on the Pill, not asking, and using a condom.

I want you.

Anata-ga hoshii. ♀
あなたが欲しい。
Kimi-ga hoshii. ♂
君が欲しい。

It's been a long time.

Hisashiburi.
久しぶり。

Love me more.

Motto aishite.
もっと愛して。

More and more.

Motto motto.
もっともっと。

Do the same thing again.

Mō ichido sō-shite.
もう1度そうして。

**How do you want me
to do it?**

Donna-fū-ni shite hoshii?
どんなふうにして欲しい？

I feel so good.

Kimochi ii.
気持ちいい。
Sugoku ii.
すごくいい。

Touch me.

Sawatte.
触って。

Bite me.

Kande.
かんで。

Stronger.

Motto tsuyoku.
もっと強く。

Softer.

Motto yasashiku.
もっと優しく。

Faster.

Motto hayaku.
もっと速く。

Slower.

Motto yukkuri.
もっとゆっくり。

Deeper.

Motto fukaku.
もっと深く。

I'm coming.

Iku iku. ♀
いくいく。
Iki-sō-da. ♂
いきそうだ。

Did you like (that)?

Yokatta?
よかった？

Did you come?

Itta?
いった？

That was good.	Yokatta. よかった。 Yokatta-yo. ♂ よかったよ。
That was wonderful.	Sugoku yokatta. すごくよかった。
One more time?	Mō ikkai? もう1回？
I don't wanna leave you.	Hanaretakunai. 離れたくない。
I wanna stay with you forever.	Zutto issho-ni itai. ずっと一緒にいたい。
Will you marry me?	Kekkon shite-kureru? 結婚してくれる？
I don't want to get married yet.	Mada kekkon shitakunai. まだ結婚したくない。
I don't want to get engaged yet.	Mada konyaku shitakunai. まだ婚約したくない。

I don't want to think about marriage yet.	Mada kekkon-nante kangaetakunai. まだ結婚なんて考えたくない。
I love you but I can't marry you.	Suki-dakedo kekkon-wa dekinai. 好きだけど結婚はできない。
It's not time for me to get serious.	Mada maji-ni naritakunai. まだまじになりたくない。
Don't get me wrong.	Gokai shinai-de. 誤解しないで。
I need time to myself.	Jibun-no jikan-ga hitsuyō-nano.♀ 自分の時間が必要なの。 Jibun-no jikan-ga hitsuyō-nanda.♂ 自分の時間が必要なんだ。
I'm not good for you.	Atashi-wa anata-ni fusawashikunai-wa. ♀ あたしはあなたにふさわしくないわ。 Boku-wa kimi-ni fusawashikunai-yo. ♂ 僕は君にふさわしくないよ。
Forget about me.	Atashi-no-koto wasurete. ♀ あたしの事忘れて。 Boku-no-koto wasurete. ♂ 僕の事忘れて。

The Other Side

14

I'm sorry it didn't work out.

Zannen-dakedo atashi-tachi
　　awanakatta-noyo. ♀
残念だけど、あたしたち合わなかっ
　　たのよ。
Zannen-dakedo bokutachi
　　awanakattan-dayo. ♂
残念だけど、僕達合わなかったん
　　だよ。

It's over.

Mō owari-dane.
もう終わりだね。
Mō owari-da. ♂
もう終わりだ。

Don't be persistent.

Shitsukoku shinai-de. ♀
しつこくしないで。
Shitsukoku suruna-yo. ♂
しつこくするなよ。

I can't see you anymore.	Mō aenai. もう会えない。 Mō aenai-yo. もう会えないよ。
I won't call you anymore.	Mō denwa shinai. もう電話しない。
I don't love you anymore.	Mō suki janai. もう好きじゃない。
I have another girlfriend/boyfriend.	Hoka-ni kareshi-ga dekita-no. ♀ 他に彼氏ができたの。 Hoka-ni kanojo-ga dekita. ♂ 他に彼女ができた。

I'm not interested in you anymore.	Mō anata-ni kyōmi-ga nai-no. ♀ もうあなたに興味がないの。 Mō kimi-ni kyōmi-ga nain-da. ♂ もう君に興味がないんだ。
Being with you is no fun.	Issho-ni-ite, mō tano-shikunai. 一緒にいて、もう楽しくない。
You're boring!	Anata tsumannai! ♀ あなたつまんない！ Kimi tsumannē! ♂ 君つまんねえ！

Stop bothering me!

Jama shinai-deyo!
邪魔しないでよ！

Jama shinai-de-kure!
邪魔しないでくれ！

You don't love me anymore, do you?

Mō atashi-no-koto suki
  janain-deshō? ♀
もうあたしの事好きじゃないん
  でしょう？

Mō boku-no-koto suki
  janain-darō? ♂
もう僕の事好きじゃないんだろう？

Do you have another girlfriend/boyfriend?

Hoka-ni kanojo/kareshi-ga
  dekita-no?
他に彼女／彼氏ができたの？

Please tell me. I want to know.

Oshiete. Shiritai-no. ♀
教えて。知りたいの。

Oshiete. Shiritain-da. ♂
教えて。知りたいんだ。

I'm sorry I haven't been a good girlfriend/boyfriend.	Ii kanojo-janakute gomen-ne. ♀ いい彼女じゃなくてごめんね。 Ii kareshi-janakute gomen-ne. ♂ いい彼氏じゃなくてごめんね。
It's my fault.	Atashi-ga warui-no. ♀ あたしが悪いの。 Boku-no sei. ♂ 僕のせい。
Can't we start again?	Mō ichido yarinaose-nai? もう1度やり直せない？
I'm serious about you.	Anata-no-koto maji/honki-nano. ♀ あなたの事まじ／本気なの。 Kimi-no-koto maji-nanda. ♂ 君の事まじ／本気なんだ。
I can't live without you.	Anata-nashi-ja ikiteke-nai. ♀ あなたなしじゃ生きてけない。 Kimi-nashi-ja ikiteke-nai. ♂ 君なしじゃ生きてけない。
Please understand my feelings.	Atashi-no kimochi wakatte. ♀ あたしの気持ち分かって。 Boku-no kimochi wakatte. ♂ 僕の気持ち分かって。
I will never forget you.	Anata-no-koto wasure-nai. ♀ あなたの事忘れない。 Kimi-no-koto wasure-nai. ♂ 君の事忘れない。
Thanks for the beautiful memories.	Ii omoide-o arigatō. いい思い出をありがとう。
I'm so happy to have known you.	Shiriaete/Deaete yokatta. 知り合えて／出合えてよかった。

Remember me sometimes.	Tokidoki atashi-no-koto omoidashite. ♀ 時々あたしの事思い出して。 Tokidoki boku-no-koto omoidashite. ♂ 時々僕の事思い出して。
Can we still be friends?	Mada tomodachi-de irareru? まだ友達でいられる？
Be happy with her/him.	Kanojo/kare-to shiawase-nine. 彼女・彼と幸せにね。
I loved you.	Aishiteta. ♀ 愛してた。 Aishiteta-yo. ♂ 愛してたよ。
I will always love you.	Zutto anata-o omotteru. ♀ ずっとあなたを思ってる。 Zutto kimi-o omotteru. ♂ ずっと君を思ってる。

I really don't love you anymore, so I'm going to change my phone number.	Mō suki janai-kara, denwa bangō kaeru. もう好きじゃないから電話番号変える。
By the way, how much does a Japanese wedding cost?	Tokoro-de, Nihon-no kekkon-shikitte ikura-kakaru-no? ところで、日本の結婚式っていくらかかるの？
Forget it!	Yameta! 止めた！
I'll miss you.	Sabishikunaru-yo. 寂しくなるよ。
I'll always think of you.	Itsumo anata-o omotteru/kangaeteru-wa. ♀ いつもあなたを思ってる／考えてるわ。 Itsumo kimi-o omotteru/kangaeteru-yo. ♂ いつも君を思ってる／考えてるよ。
I'll always love you.	Itsumo suki. ♀ いつも好き。 Itsumo suki-dayo. ♂ いつも好きだよ。

I'll write letters.

Tegami kaku-yo.
手紙書くよ。

Will you write me a letter?

Tegami kureru?
手紙くれる？

I'll call you from Thailand.

Tai-kara denwa suru.
タイから電話する。

I'll call you when I return.

Kaette-kitara denwa suru.
帰かえって来たら電話する。

I'll be back soon.

Sugu kaette-kuru.
すぐ帰って来る。
Sugu kaette-kuru-yo.
すぐ帰って来るよ。

Please understand.

(Dōka) wakatte.
（どうか）分かって。

I have to go because it's my job.	Shigoto dakara ikanakucha. 仕事だから行かなくちゃ。
Take care of yourself.	Genki-dene. 元気でね。
Please wait for my return.	Mattete-ne. 待っててね。

You can use this anytime—when leaving your house, going to the restroom, getting a drink at the bar...

Don't cry.	Nakanai-de. 泣かないで。
Wipe your tears.	Namida fuite. 涙ふいて。

I can't stand it!	Gaman dekinai! 我慢できない！ Gaman dekinai-yo! 我慢できないよ！ Taerarenai! たえられない！

Taerarenai-yo!
たえられないよ！

All of these phrases can be used for both sad and mad feelings.

It's difficult for me too.   Atashi-mo tsurai-wa. ♀
あたしも辛いわ。

Boku-mo tsurain-da. ♂
僕も辛いんだ。